THE LAW OF CONSERVATION OF VALUE

THE LAW OF CONSERVATION OF VALUE

Nick Harkiolakis

Hult International Business School, USA

NEW JERSEY · LONDON · SINGAPORE · BEIJING · SHANGHAI · HONG KONG · TAIPEI · CHENNAI · TOKYO

Published by

World Scientific Publishing Europe Ltd.

57 Shelton Street, Covent Garden, London WC2H 9HE

Head office: 5 Toh Tuck Link, Singapore 596224

USA office: 27 Warren Street, Suite 401-402, Hackensack, NJ 07601

Library of Congress Control Number: 2025011787

British Library Cataloguing-in-Publication Data
A catalogue record for this book is available from the British Library.

THE LAW OF CONSERVATION OF VALUE

ISBN 978-1-80061-743-8 (hardcover)
ISBN 978-1-80061-744-5 (ebook for institutions)
ISBN 978-1-80061-745-2 (ebook for individuals)

For any available supplementary material, please visit
https://www.worldscientific.com/worldscibooks/10.1142/Q0513#t=suppl

Desk Editors: Nambirajan Karuppiah/Gabriel Rawlinson

Typeset by Stallion Press
Email: enquiries@stallionpress.com

PREFACE

An attempt is made in this book to provide a framework for dealing with economic concepts that closely resemble conservation laws but with economic variables. The economic variable of value is considered here as conserved throughout transactions between agents. Using value as a quantity that can be accumulated and exchanged among actors and as an encapsulation of various economic variables such as utility and labor allowed for the development of the law of conservation of value. While abstracting at this high level might seem like an intellectual exercise, the conclusions drawn can be useful in dealing with some of the theoretical and practical challenges economists are facing.

A framework is the foundational blueprint upon which one can develop concepts and theories that comply with certain principles. In our case here, this principle is the law of conservation of value. We need to emphasize here that with value we mean something of value to us or humans. This view should also be seen as specific to the individual, group, organization, and government. What is of value to one individual might not be of the same value or even of any value to another. Value is subjective and always depends on the point of view of the interested party.

Although a proper definition of value and its proxies will be provided, in the context of this book and in simplified terms, value is anything that is significant to someone. In this respect, value can equate to wealth in terms of possessions (clothes, houses, cars, money, etc.), physical health in terms of strength to accomplish something, intellectual potential in terms of our intellectual capacity, knowledge, and skills, and emotional satisfaction in terms of addressing our needs and self-actualization. The notion of money as value is seen here as future value, which is the potential to act and engage in transactions with other agents. When we have money, we can buy something (gain value) in a future instance in time, whether that instance is in one second, one month, or one year. Seen as future value, we can easily attribute gains and losses according to the transactions involved. If that money were to be invested in the stock market, its value could in the future increase or decrease according to the performance of the stock we chose.

While the choice of the word value is meant to emphasize the anthropocentric notion of the term, there is nothing preventing us from attaching it to other forms of inanimate and animate entities. For example, nature can be seen as an agent with unlimited wealth but zero physical and intellectual needs. This is the convenient assumption for most of the economic analyses in the past that contradicts the modern perspective where nature is viewed as a limited pool of resources that need to be preserved as much as possible.

This book is organized into five chapters with the first one dedicated to the development of the framework and law of conservation of value with its theoretical foundation and its mathematical expression. In order to get right to the point, a historical account of the concept of value has been moved to Appendix. Its existence is for the inquiring reader and for completeness purposes as it connects the past with the present. This way the real contribution of the concepts presented here is immediately accessible from the beginning of the book.

Chapter 2 focuses on the application of the law of conservation of value in the market, and Chapter 3 does the same for the case of the economy and government. While examples in both conceptual and numerical forms are considered throughout the book, a special mention of potential applications of the law of conservation of value with proxies of value is considered in Chapter 4. Value as capital, utility, goods, and information is discussed in the chapter. An additional section explores value as a need with a hierarchy of needs at its core.

Finally, Chapter 5 introduces the analogy between physical and economic sciences with respect to the cycle of value and the law of conservation of value. It should be noted that in all chapters, the demonstrations of the law of conservation of value are kept as "light" as possible for the benefit of the lay reader. Occasionally, more in-depth analysis is considered for the purposes of validating the law of conservation of value in a specific context. The academic reader should be able to modify and expand the findings to suit their research. For the policymaker, the value could be in the insights the law of conservation provides and its applicability for developing government and institutional policies.

ABOUT THE AUTHOR

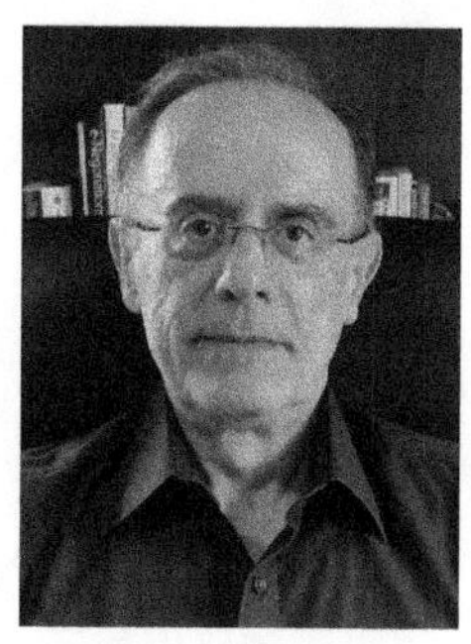 **Nicholas Harkiolakis** is Vice President for Europe and the Middle East and Director of Research at Executive Coaching Consultants. He is Editor of the *International Journal of Teaching and Case Studies* and Associate Editor of the *International Journal of Social Entrepreneurship and Innovation*. He is the author of the *Quantitative Research Methods: From Theory to Publication* textbook and the research books *e-Negotiations: Networking and Cross-Cultural Business Transactions, Multipreneurship: Diversification in Times of Crisis,* and *Leadership Explained: Leading Teams in the 21st Century*. He is a Professor at Hult International Business School and also teaches graduate courses and supervises dissertations at various universities in France, the UK, and the US.

CONTENTS

LIST OF FIGURES

1

THE CONSERVATION OF VALUE

One of the most challenging concepts in economics since the first accounts of economic thought is that of value. Defining it is difficult, primarily due to its subjective nature, at least as perceived by individuals, organizations, and societies. Individuals have different perceptions of the value of a piece of art, friendship, chocolate, clean air, democracy, relaxing by the beach, owning a yacht, watching a good movie, being healthy, life after death, etc.

If some of the options in the previous list might sound extreme, keep in mind that whole institutions such as governments, religions, and societies capitalize on them for their mere existence. Value can be seen as a measure of appreciation for something, a monetary worth, benefit, usefulness, etc., relative to something that is not presumably at its desired level or missing completely. In this sense, value is more like beauty, which is in the eyes of the beholder since it requires an outside observer for its existence. This subjective observer, for all purposes, could be any living entity or group of entities dependent on their environment for survival and growth.

Written accounts debating the definition of value can be traced as far back as the fourth century BC, when Aristotle distinguished between the value of "use" and the value of "exchange". One could value their clothing because of their function/use (keeping them warm and protected from the elements) but also could exchange them if needed for food or services with another who was interested in having them. After this initial treatment, it took until medieval times (13th century AD) for Aquinas and Scotus to give value an ethical flavor as something one deserves and can receive by producing work that could result in a product or service.

From then on, and starting from the 17th century, a race to define value has been taking place in attempts to equate it with utility, labor, land, market price, and various combinations and subdivisions of these. Along the way, the dynamic influence of time became evident, and concepts such as supply and demand and marginal utility surfaced in an attempt to explain the behavior of businesses, markets, and economies at large. While the reductionist approach to defining value has produced a number of breakthroughs, the economic challenges we face today are an indication that we haven't really managed to develop a theory of value, at least as successfully as other concepts in hard sciences such as physics, chemistry, and mathematics.

Value is an abstract construct that has no physical manifestation. It does not exist in the physical world, at least as an observable physical entity, and for that reason it cannot be sensed or detected through our senses or instruments. Nevertheless, its existence in language makes it an information-carrying element that is ordinal in nature, meaning we can order it along a continuum from low to high. As such, it is suitable for comparisons and, as we will see later, for arithmetic manipulation.

Estimating value is an integral part of our lives, playing a role in shaping our priorities and preferences. Even reading this book is a value process. Consequently, the hierarchy of values we adopt guides our decisions and the way we position ourselves in our interactions with everything around us. Our plans of action and the strategies we form to reach our goals are themselves estimations of value relative to our hierarchies of values.

A contradiction between the assumptions of traditional economics and the realities of the market results in much of the inequalities and inefficiencies we observe in today's societies. The core contradiction is the assumption of equal levels of rationality among individual agents and their competition as the judge of market direction. If everyone is equal (even in terms of rationality), how can it be possible to have some who are winners and others who are losers? The answer lies in every other factor that plays a role in what happens, including the operational environment and resources available. Even this consideration is not going to work; therefore, the primary assumption of equal rationality is a false premise that does not reflect reality.

Another assumption in traditional economics is that market outcomes are fair and equitable. The increasing divide between the poor and the rich would beg to differ. Finally, the notion of "free choice" is prevalent in traditional economics. Social unrests and inequalities again will beg to differ on how "free" someone's choice is given the constraints imposed in many cases. How free is a person to choose the education they want when they are poor?

Under the current circumstances, on our resource-limited planet, if everyone were to be wealthy, there would need to be fewer people, and we would require robots/slaves to provide labor. A master–slave duality seems to be a precondition of wealth. If we want everyone on Earth to be wealthy, then, considering the population growth we are experiencing, we will need a few more Earths to sustain us.

Before we get into a more substantive discussion of the societal challenges of economic thought, it is worth mentioning here that the challenges are not only conceptual and philosophical but also pragmatic in the sense of lacking tools to express the problems we observe and subsequently solve. For example, the premise of maximizing wealth is wrong, simply because it refers to some sort of total – or in some cases, an average – that we need to increase.

Both of those metrics can lead to misrepresentations since they do not consider our values regarding human life and life in general. Total wealth could skyrocket, giving the impression of an affluent society, only to realize that this society is composed of few "masters" and many "slaves". Similarly, the average of wealth might be increasing due to some "rich" outliers, while much of the population is poor. Both metrics in the previous examples indicate a wealthy but inhumane society. What is missing in this view is a measure of "humanness" that balances the concept of wealth or a new metric that more realistically represents the health of a society or economy.

1.1 The Cycle of Value

Let's consider the simplistic case of a meadow where sheep run wild and graze the grass in a random fashion and as they please (right-hand side of Figure 1.1). Then, humans come and start corralling the sheep into an enclosed space. The question that concerns economics is why they did so when they could just as well milk, shear, and eat them where they were. The answer is simply because it is more valuable or convenient to have the sheep corralled where you can easily access and exploit them for their milk, wool, and meat. We should note here that, although the number of sheep was the same in both the field and the corral, the latter arrangement is more valuable to us humans than the former. An economist would say that we produced entropy (more on this later), but that would be misusing a physics term devised to measure disorder. A physicist would say that, while the sheep in the field and those in the corral have the same energy (equal in numbers), the ones in the field have higher disorder or entropy than those in the corral. So, what we did by corralling the sheep, from the point of view of physics, is reduce the entropy of the sheep (seen as a system here), so we can control its release. The economist would describe this process as the production of entropy. Now, why the physicist sees something as a reduction while the economist sees it as a production or increase is a contextual preference. The former is trying to see things from the perspective of an objective, outside observer, while the latter sees things from the perspective of purpose and its potential for human exploitation.

Figure 1.1. The beginning of the case.

Looking at what we described in more detail, we can say that there was something of value out there (in nature), we exerted some effort to collect and organize it, and we ended up with something that is more valuable to us than before. Granted, we spend some energy and sweat to go and collect the sheep, but we can easily envision the possibilities and benefits of our new situation. We also might have used some rope or special shoes and clothes to run in the field and chase the sheep (we could even use a trained dog). With some effort again (and extra sweating) and using different tools, we can easily convert what we have in produce (milk, wool, and meat) and make some money by selling it. Figure 1.2 depicts the process we just described by representing the labor/capital we spend with the dollar sign and the energy/effort we lost in the process with the explosion graphic. Our goal, through the whole process (excluding other factors), is to hopefully end up with more money than we started.

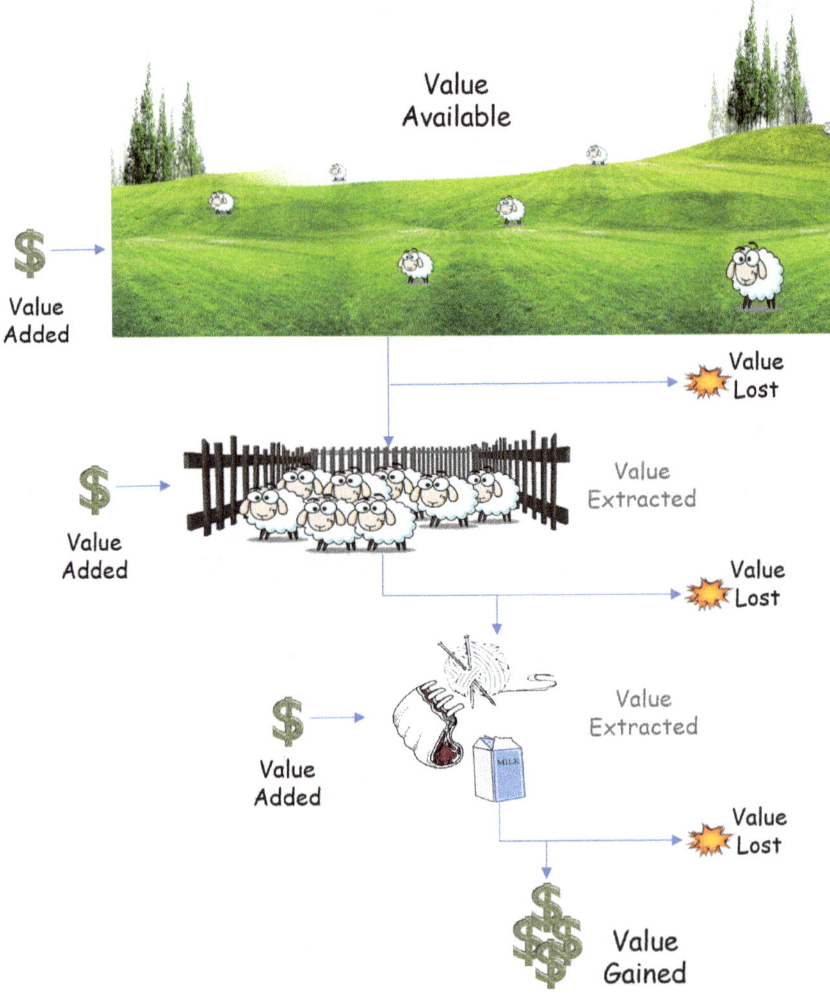

Figure 1.2.   The value creation process.

In economics, as in any other science, it helps to abstract the phenomena we observe as much as possible to simplify their complexity to a level that is easy to express in formulas and develop theories to describe them. Abstractions also allow us to generalize our descriptions and findings to wider domains. It is easy to imagine that what we described with sheep can be easily applied to other livestock (fish, birds, etc.) and natural resources. In that respect, Figure 1.2 can be seen as a special case of the more general process depicted in Figure 1.3, where the various components of the process are represented as tanks of a "magical" fluid called *value*. The choice of the word "value" here was made to emphasize the anthropogenic approach we are following in studying what is called the production process. The subjective connotations of the word will be addressed later when we present the consumer and producer perspectives. Hereafter, we accept the term "value" as an all-encompassing concept similar to the adage "beauty is in the eye of the beholder". In our case it will be *value is in the mind of the beholder*. The beholder, in this case, is any social entity (individual, group, organization, or state/government).

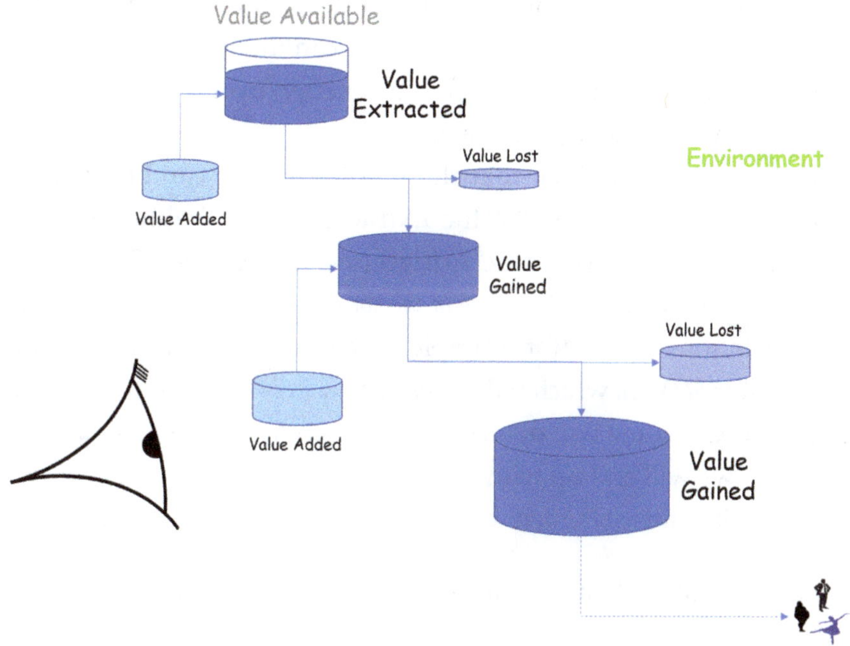

Figure 1.3.   The conceptualized value creation process.

We see value as representative of a process within the physical and social worlds. In this respect, value is not something that exists in an instance of time independently of its past or future; rather, it is the culmination of an agent's activities when interacting with the natural and social environments. In other words, it is a potential to act in a situation. As a working definition, value can be seen as *the potential to act in an environment.*

While the extracted and gained values will be seen as static or state elements, the added and lost values will be seen more as dynamic or flowing elements (changes in static elements). This conjecture will hopefully become clearer at the end of the book when we compare the conservation of value with the law of conservation of energy. As "Value Added", we consider everything that went into the process, including money (seen here as a proxy for inherited, borrowed, and accumulated value from past transactions), labor, and equity of any other form that is suitable for an exchange. As "Value Lost", we consider anything that cannot be returned to the cycle if it were to be repeated, including energy (mainly heat), money (transaction costs, debt), and waste.

We can easily deduce that the whole process can be seen as a balance sheet between "Value Extracted" and "Value Gained" through exchanges of Value Added and Value Lost. Figure 1.4 depicts what we will call *the law of the conservation of value.* The value that exists somewhere (for example, in nature) requires an amount of *Value Added* (VA), which will be used to access *Value Extracted* (VE). In the process, some will dissipate into the environment as *Value Lost* (VL), and we will end up with a net amount of *Value Gained* (VG). We can formulate this statement as

"Value Added" + "Value Extracted" = "Value Lost" + "Value Gained"

and, in acronym form,

$$VA + VE = VL + VG \tag{1.1}$$

What the equation describes is the transformation of value. A visual representation of the law is depicted in Figure 1.4, where the scale indicates the balance between the two sides of the equation. The balancing of values can be seen taking place at various stages of the transformation or production process and can even be applied additively across multiple steps or cycles of the process.

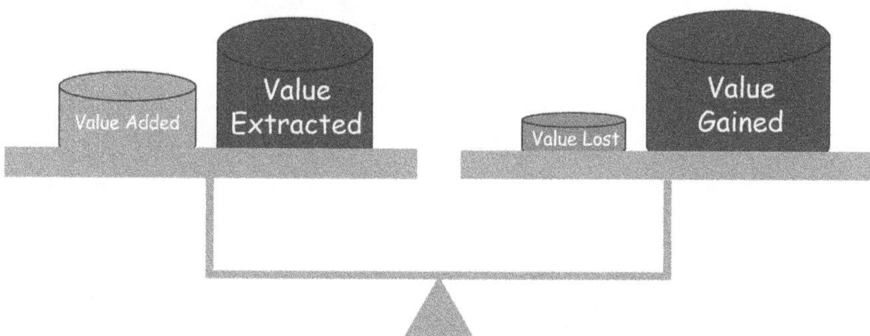

Figure 1.4. The law of conservation of value.

The continuous process in Figure 1.3 eventually ends (hopefully) with the distribution of more value to society or at least parts of it. For some, the outcome will be material for their immediate needs in the form of food, clothing, entertainment, etc., while for others, it will be in the form of money or profit. The latter is interesting because it is not value in the typical sense of present value but rather credit for value they can claim in the future. This idea of value reserves that can be used in the future is one of the cornerstones of modern economics and a characteristic of human societies.

Considering the notion of crossing past, present, and future in terms of value flow, one can borrow value from the future (for example, by borrowing from a bank), do their production magic in the present, and, when the future becomes present, return it with interest (Figure 1.5). Danger lurks in the unpredictable nature of the future, which brings uncertainties with respect to our ability to effectively break even the balance sheet of values.

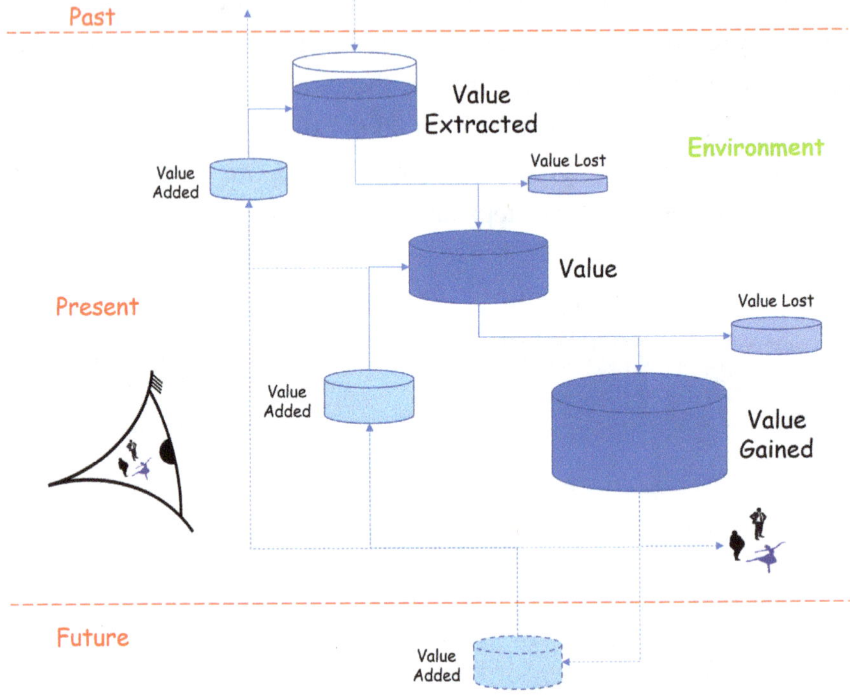

Figure 1.5. The value creation process over time.

To avoid losing our grip on economic reality, Figure 1.6 presents a duplicate of Figure 1.5, but with value labels replaced with their appropriate economic terms or jargon for the readers who are more comfortable seeing such terms. The value added that we have mentioned so far is typically referred to as capital or labor. Capital is nothing more than a token or proxy of labor that can be engaged in an exchange at will. Someone who has money can hire a shepherd, a butcher, or any other skilled individual required to complete the process illustrated in Figure 1.2; therefore, capital is nothing more than the potential to release labor for an activity. An economist might see value as revenue in the form of the quantity of items or products multiplied by their price. Every arrow in Figure 1.6 connects the supply of something to its demand.

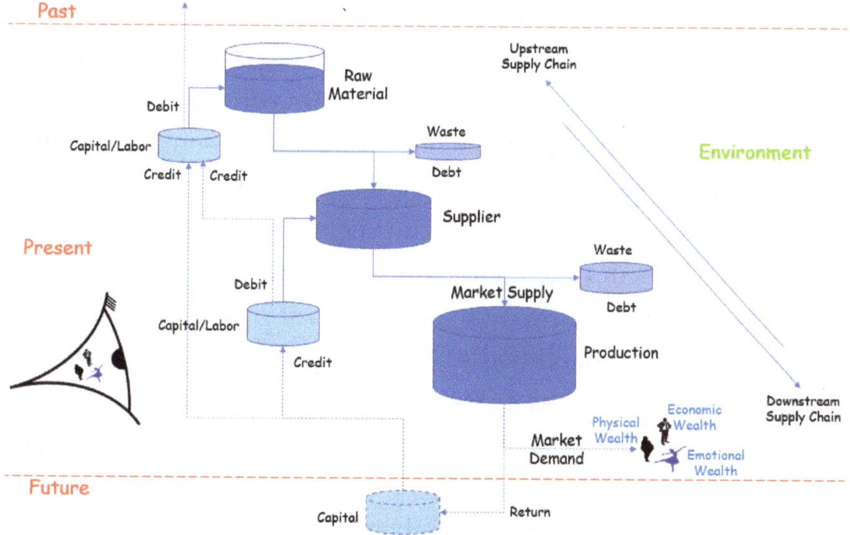

Figure 1.6. The value creation process over time in "economic lingo".

An economic concept that might sound similar to *value* is that of *utility*, or, more specifically, that of *marginal utility*. It is assumed in traditional economics that the goal of individuals – and by extension, that of their organizations and societies – is to increase their pleasure or happiness, as modeled by utility. In that sense, utility became equivalent to wealth, which is a form of accumulated value. A crucial assumption here is that maximization of utility drives decision-making. This assumption presumes a dynamic nature where equilibrium, in terms of optimal changes, is possible and desirable. Everyone is "happy" together, although if someone takes risks, they may become happier than others. Game theory literally epitomizes this premise.

The reason the word "value" was preferred over "utility" in this book is simply to avoid the association of utility with utilitarianism and its moral connotations that would assume an intention to fair and just distribution of utility or wealth. This contradicts the free-market realities that are better reflected as the survival of the fittest. With respect to *marginal utility* (adding satisfaction or usefulness), the assumption of seeking to marginalize (maximize) something is suggestive of our intention to increase it by adding something extra. This direction will make the notion of equilibrium an antagonistic battlefield, where opponents reach a stalemate, and no one can gain more than others despite their continuous efforts. In this book, we look at the economic situation as a constant flow of value where its conservation is established as "law". In other words, we see our coexistence with nature as a closed system in which its total value is preserved, while internally it can be distributed differently. Looking at Earth as a spaceship in the vacuum of the cosmos is probably the best analogy of what is considered in this book a closed system of value or a system with a finite amount of value.

Considering the previous images, we could intuitively see a cyclic process of the flow and conversion of value. VA and VE work together to produce VG and VL. The produced VG can then be consumed or used as VA for another cycle of conversion or production. Figure 1.7 depicts what we will call here the *cycle of value*. This analogy will be used in future sections to explain the economic perspectives of governments, organizations, and even individuals as they engage in economic activities. While the analogy to a great extent follows the systems theory concepts of stocks and flows, it will be shown here how it differs from them significantly.

The cycle of value is an alternative visualization of the law of conservation of value (Figure 1.4). It will henceforth be used as a more appealing representation of the law due to its simplicity and the inherent notion that value creation is a repeated process. Something that should not be confused is that the representation of Figure 1.7 is not a sequence in time in which we first add the value, then extract it, then lose some, and eventually end up with some. The cycle is dynamic in that we add and lose value continually from beginning to end. Figure 1.7 and equation (1.1) describe the accounting of the

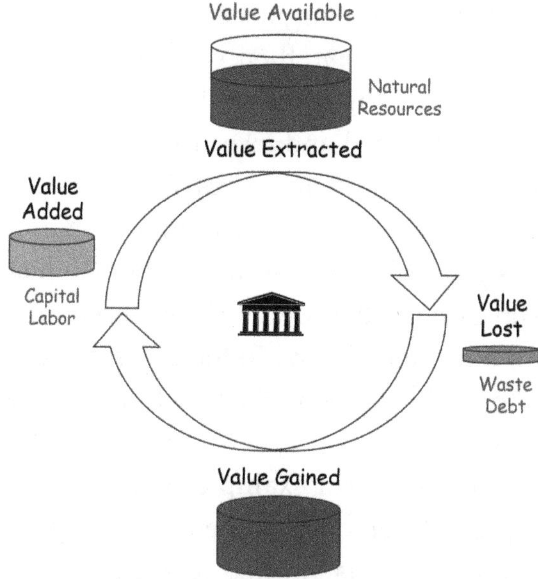

Figure 1.7. The cycle of value.

elements, similarly to how profits and losses on a balance sheet are accumulated figures for gains and losses throughout a year. The time element is not apparent, but we will soon see how it can be introduced.

Having a cycle that leads to more cycles, and when multiple entities access the VE, it could intuitively suggest that some coordination and control will be required so things do not get out of hand. This is where government and political institutions with regulations and control mechanisms come into the picture (Figure 1.7). A government's role is to ensure that this cyclical transformation keeps moving in the right direction (clockwise in our case) so that citizens can continue and prosper in an ever-increasing way. In return, the government will take a share of the VG for its future functions and leave the remainder to the individuals and organizations that invested in the process. Chapter 3 is dedicated to discussing the role of government in the cycle of value.

If we suspect that there might be something wrong with an increase in value *ad infinitum*, then we are heading in the right direction of acknowledging some of the challenges our societies face today. Moved by greed and insecurities, we might be slowly reaching a point where natural resources (the container that is called nature or Planet Earth) become scarce for any significant growth to occur. This is probably the first time in human history that we have been so obsessed with growth that we need to see further in the future than our predecessors. In the process, we seem to have developed a shortsightedness on the belief that our ingenuity will make sure things go well too.

While practical numerical examples will be discussed in the upcoming chapters, I demonstrate here some aspects of the law of conservation of value as applied to economic theory. Let us first consider exports and exchange rates. In this case, we assume a manufacturer that wants to export products to countries with a different currency from where they are produced. Let us assume that an amount of goods of value β_0 is produced. This will represent the *Value Added* to the cycle of value. Given an exchange rate of say r and assuming a steady increase of exported goods β_1 for every increase of the exchange rate by 1, then the *Value Extracted* can be expressed as $\beta_1 \times r$. As the cycle evolves, there would be some losses (in this case due to uncertainties) equal to an amount u. This is the *Value Lost* in the cycle. Finally, we represent the *Value Gained* with X.

In this case, equation (1.1) becomes

$$VA + VE = VL + VG$$

or

$$\beta_0 + \beta_1 \times r = u + X$$

or

$$X = \beta_0 + \beta_1 \times r - u$$

This is one of the simplest forms of an export-and-exchange rate equation that financial stakeholders use to analyze and forecast trade patterns, make policy decisions, and inform business strategies. Because, in most cases, we don't know the direction of the term u, it tends to appear as $+u$ in most expressions of the previous equation. If we are interested in using it for multiple cycles, then we can introduce the index i to identify specific cycles, as in

$$X_i = \beta_0 + \beta_1 \times r_i - u$$

Another example relates unemployment and inflation, where lower unemployment in an economy is associated with higher inflation, and vice versa. We will develop the corresponding equations in Chapter 3.

1.2 Marginal Value

In this section, some mathematical formulas are developed that derive from the law of conservation of value. First, we introduce the rate of change of value and its corresponding economic term. Many physical quantities are expressed as rates of change, including velocity or speed, which is the rate of change of distance with time, and power, which is the rate of change of energy with time. In mathematical formalism, rates of change are considered instantaneous, which means time tends to be as small as possible (i.e., tends toward zero) and expressed as the first derivative of the variable they represent with respect to time. In relation to the cycle of value we study here and considering value as the variable of interest, the velocity of value is nothing more than the rate of change of value over time. Here, we refer to this quantity as *marginal value* in relation to the concept of marginal utility in economics.

The difference between the two is that marginal value represents the rate of change over time, while marginal utility represents the rate of change of quantity produced. To be more precise, economists like to think of marginal utility as the increase in utility when an additional unit of output is achieved. With a steady flow of production, as standard economics assumes, there will be a direct correspondence between the unit of production and the time it takes to produce it, making marginal value similar to marginal utility. We will see here that considering time as our independent variable offers advantages in terms of expressiveness in economic terms.

Before we move further, it is worth mentioning here that the "law" of marginal utility and the law of "diminishing marginal utility" that we will see later are not based on any mathematical formulation or proof that is confirmed by a hypothesis testing process. They are propositions that are true by the very nature of humans engaging in either voluntary or coerced exchanges, where they try to maximize their utility. They assume that rationally acting individuals always try to maximize satisfaction or utility. In other words, between two satisfying alternatives, one will always choose the option that provides more satisfaction.

For the following discussion, we use the Lagrange notation to indicate the derivative of a variable (x') instead of the Leibniz (dx/dt) form. Let's consider first that for a short time interval or unit of time (dt tends to zero), a Marginal Value Added (VA′) has been injected into the cycle and accessed a Marginal Value Extracted (VE′). In the process, a Marginal Value Lost (VL′) is lost. As a result, we will end up with Marginal Value Gained (VG′) (Figure 1.8). By differentiating (1.1), we get

$$(VA + VE)' = (VL + VG)'$$

or

$$VA' + VE' = VL' + VG'$$

or

$$VG' = VA' + VE' - VL'$$

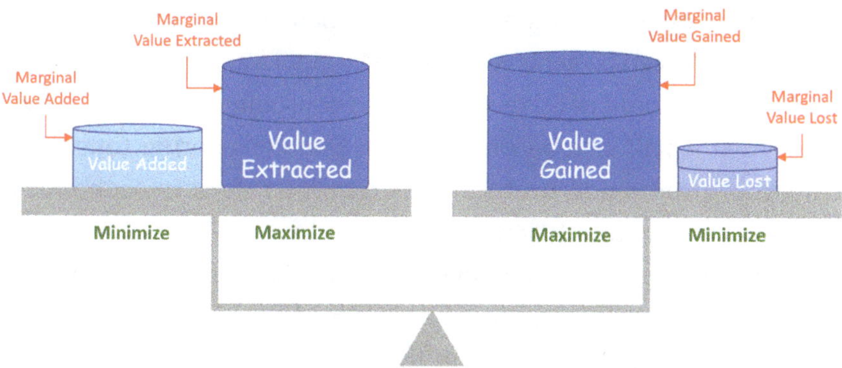

Figure 1.8. The balance of marginal values.

Our goal in economics would be to maximize our gains and minimize our losses. If we assume an abundant source of extracted value, like nature according to neoclassical economics, then the rate of the extracted value would be zero simply because the amount of value in nature will not change. This assumption is not far-fetched at least when one considers small time horizons such as months and years. Moving into decades, things might get a little riskier, and for certain, moving into centuries and millennia, the assumption is bound to fail given the limited size and resources of Earth.

The last equation then becomes

$$VG' = VA' - VL' \tag{1.2}$$

This means that the Marginal Value Gained will be equal to the Marginal Value Added minus the Marginal Value Lost. Considering that the goal of agents is to maximize their Value Gained, then $VG' = 0$ when the maximum of Value Gained is reached. In this case, (1.2) becomes

$$VA' = VL' \tag{1.3}$$

The maximization of Marginal Value Gained (i.e., a faster rate of gaining value) can be achieved when Marginal Value Added is equal to Marginal Value Lost. We will see the consequences of this result later when it will also become evident that considering time rates instead of production unit rates, as currently used in economics, results in more naturally interpretable results.

What we applied for one cycle can also be applied to multiple cycles running simultaneously by simply adding the various components. Equation (1.2) will then suggest that the sum of the Marginal Value Gained through all cycles is equal to the sum of the Marginal Value Added minus the sum of Marginal Value Lost. Similarly, (1.3) will suggest that to maximize our gains, we need to make sure that the sum of the Marginal Value Added is equal to the sum of Marginal Value Lost.

1.3 Rate of Change of Marginal Value

Having considered the velocity or rate of change in time (marginal value) during the cycle of value, the next step would be to consider acceleration, which is the rate of change of velocity. The equivalent concept in economics is that of diminishing marginal utility, which is defined as the rate of decline of marginal utility. For some reason, "diminishing" is more popular in economics than the opposite, "increasing" (for lack of a better antonym), probably because it represents trouble that requires attention. For example, when consumption increases, producers seem to be happy and don't see the need for any action, while when consumption decreases, producers will start losing money unless they act to reduce production or take other measures such as promotions or lowering prices to increase sales.

So, in the case of the cycle of value, we will use the term "Speed of Marginal Value" to denote the acceleration of value. Alternatively, the reader can use *Diminishing Marginal Value* when the rate of change of marginal value is negative (value flow decelerates) and *Increasing*

Marginal Value when the rate of change of marginal value is positive (value flow accelerates). The latter case is also of interest, as it could reveal missed opportunities for faster rates of growth. Considering the law of conservation of value in terms of the speed of change of marginal value, we will have that the Speed of Marginal Value Added (VA″) will affect the Speed of Marginal Value Extracted (VE″), and as a result it will impact the Speed of Marginal Value Gained (VG″) and the Speed of Marginal Value Lost (VL″). Using mechanical terms, the acceleration of the VA plus the acceleration of the VE is equal to the acceleration of the VL plus the acceleration of the VG. This can be expressed as

$$VA'' + VE'' = VL'' + VG''$$

or

$$VG'' = VA'' + VE'' - VL'' \tag{1.4}$$

The Speed of Marginal Value Gained is equal to the Speed of Marginal Value Added plus the Speed of Marginal Value Extracted minus the Speed of Marginal Value Lost. If we were to consider increases, then (1.4) can be interpreted as the Increasing Marginal Value Gained being equal to the Increasing Marginal Value Added plus the Increasing Marginal Value Extracted minus the Increasing Marginal Value Lost. For decreases in speed, we can use "Diminishing" instead of "Increasing".

The graph at the bottom of Figure 1.9 showcases the relationship between value, marginal value (velocity or rate of change of value), and increasing/decreasing marginal value (acceleration or rate of change of marginal value) for a sinusoidal expression of acceleration. The interpretation above the graph (ignoring the V‴ row for now) is meant to indicate the form of change in value during the corresponding changes in its velocity and acceleration. Change can be implemented by a government through, for example, an injection of money into its economy. If anything, it shows that whatever you do, the fastest growth in value is observed when its rate of change is convex. We will see what that means in Chapter 3, where we will discuss the role of the government.

The second derivative (acceleration) with respect to quantity is where economics usually ends. Considering the third derivative has not yet become mainstream. In physics, though, the situation is different as the third derivative is typically seen as a *jolt* or *jerk*. Since there is no "marginal jolt" in economics, we only focus on the *jolt of value*, which we can define here as the rate of change of the acceleration of value. This is like a kick or jumpstart in the cycle of value. It could be a sudden infusion or injection of value into the cycle, similar to monetary infusions that governments make to jump-start their economies. Examples include stimulus checks to consumers or sudden taxation when the government wants to remove value from the economy.

Equation (1.4), in terms of "Jolt Value", will become

$$VG''' = VA''' + VE''' - VL'''$$

Before delving further into the usefulness and application of the variables discussed up to now in the cycle of value, it is worth having a visual appreciation of how these terms relate and how they can be interpreted when a certain equation for the expression of value is considered. Value, up to now, has been seen as a generic term that represents something that can be exchanged and stored. The tables in Figure 1.9 display the velocity (V'), acceleration (V''), and jolt (V''') of value in terms of their signs and the interpretations that they imply.

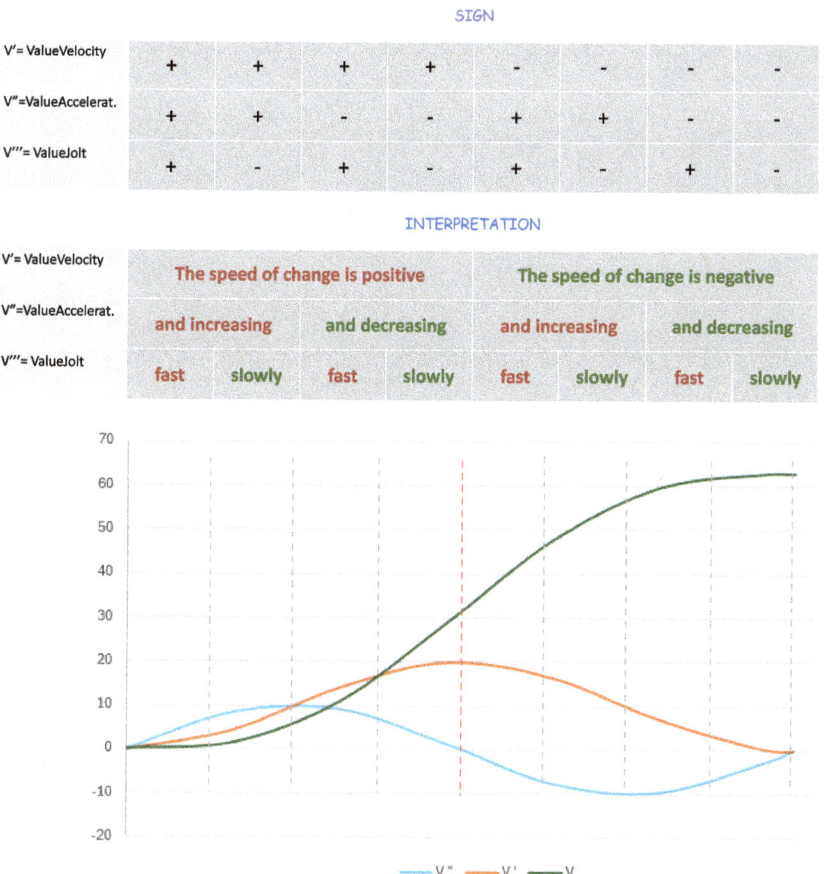

V' = ValueVelocity	+	+	+	+	-	-	-	-
V" = ValueAccelerat.	+	+	-	-	+	+	-	-
V''' = ValueJolt	+	-	+	-	+	-	+	-

	The speed of change is positive				The speed of change is negative			
and increasing		and decreasing		and increasing		and decreasing	
fast	slowly	fast	slowly	fast	slowly	fast	slowly

Figure 1.9.   Value motion variables.

In closing this chapter, it is worth pointing out that the rates of change, which refer to differentiation, have their equivalent "inverse" as integration. When we are interested in calculating the total value during a period where multiple runs of the cycle of value take place, we can use the integration of the formula adopted for value. This discussion is left for a future publication.

2

THE MARKET

The accessible universe that resources and needs form is traditionally called "the market" (Figure 2.1). This is like the physical environment, but in a more abstract form and can include physical resources as well as products and services created by humans and available to everyone with access to the market. Traditionally, economists view the market as a black box, where a kind of "magical" process called competition moves things around until a balance is achieved between prices and quantities. In that perspective, supply and demand are the forces that give life to the market. This is not a bad perspective as we do the same (at least the theorists among us) with the physical world when we try to explain it and predict its function in terms of science, instead of assuming a God-like creator and controller. Our evolution and achievements stand a testament to this process.

A critical aspect of a market is that at any single moment in time, only a fixed number of resources is available. This creates a situation known as scarcity, which in simple terms means that people (some or many) cannot afford to satisfy their needs (nowadays mainly higher order) with what they have to offer (like money or labor). This is not to be confused with shortages as the latter implies the destruction of limited supply of goods and services due to disasters (natural, such as hurricanes or flood, or man-made, such as wars, over-farming, and over-mining). Scarcity is a persistent or ongoing condition in markets. This is because resources (such as time, money, and raw materials) have multiple potential uses, and those uses compete with

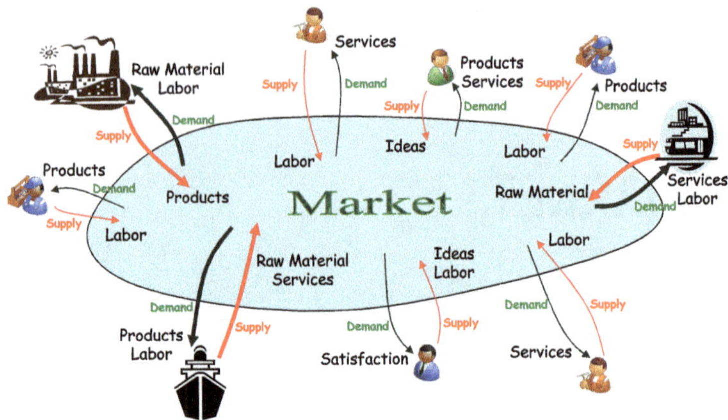

Figure 2.1.   The market environment.

each other. Since there are limited resources but many ways they can be used, scarcity remains a fundamental aspect of how markets operate. It highlights the idea that not all wants or needs can be met simultaneously because resources are finite. Land, capital, and labor, for example, could become scarcities due to growth in certain fields and territories over others. Nowadays, technology also tends to be considered as scarcity because it affects the use of land and labor to develop, manufacture, and distribute products and services more efficiently.

The trade-offs of goods and services form the economic activity that our modern societies are engaged in. Typical exchanges involve sacrificing income to buy a product, such as a laptop or a mobile phone. Exchanges take place in time and space, and in that respect, one chooses to invest their time and space in one activity over another, making the single next best alternative to the chosen one the opportunity cost. This is like the difference in value we place between activities. Provided our current choice is more valuable than the second-best alternative, one would be better off considering the current choice as gains over the alternative, instead of as opportunity cost simply because cost is mainly associated with expense or loss.

The market in that sense acts like an exchange of goods and services between producers and consumers, similar to the way the physical world acts as an exchange of forces and energy between its different entities. Of course, all market activities do take place in some physical location, whether this is a stock market or online (on a server), but for all purposes seeing it as concept space makes it much easier to represent. Prices are traditionally considered the decision mechanisms by which exchanges between sellers and buyers take place. In the traditional economic sense, prices refer to monetary values, while in the more expanded view of the market or economy that we will adopt here, prices can only be seen as potential proxies of value and an aspect of the exchange with other forms like power, satisfaction, and pleasure among them also affecting exchanges. If one would wish to deal with monetary prices only, the utility of the other types of exchange will have to be converted to price if we are to accurately represent an exchange. For example, buying a jewel could mean a lot more than the price we pay for it, for example, in the case of a wedding ring that represents commitment and status, among other things.

In terms of the cycle of value, it would be easy to see that the Value Gained and Value Added are something we, as humans, gain and commit to, respectively, while Value Extracted and Value Lost are something nature provides and receives (Figure 2.2(a)). This aligns with the neoclassical economic thought where we gain wealth from an abundant nature. The cycle of value is a give and take between agents in a closed ecosystem.

From the market perspective, the roles can be seen in dyads like supplier–consumer, where one individual or organization plays the role of the economy or consumer and the other the role of nature or supplier (Figure 2.2(b)). These roles will be intertwined and, in some transactions or cycles, someone could be a supplier while in others a consumer (Figure 2.3). We discuss the supplier and consumer roles in more detail when we discuss supply and demand later.

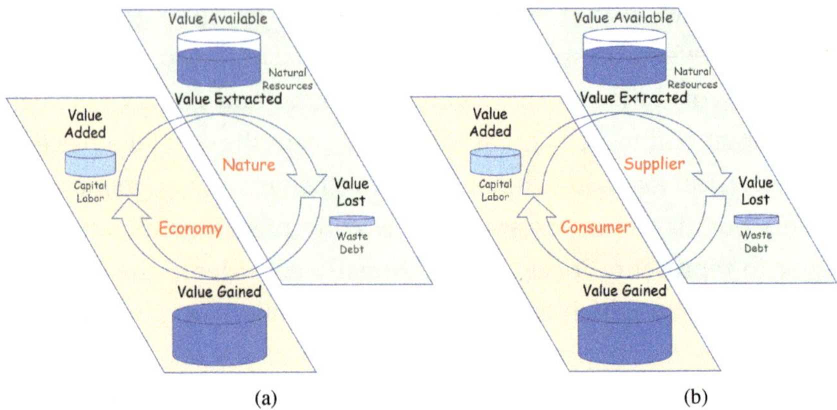

Figure 2.2. The cycle of value from an economic perspective.

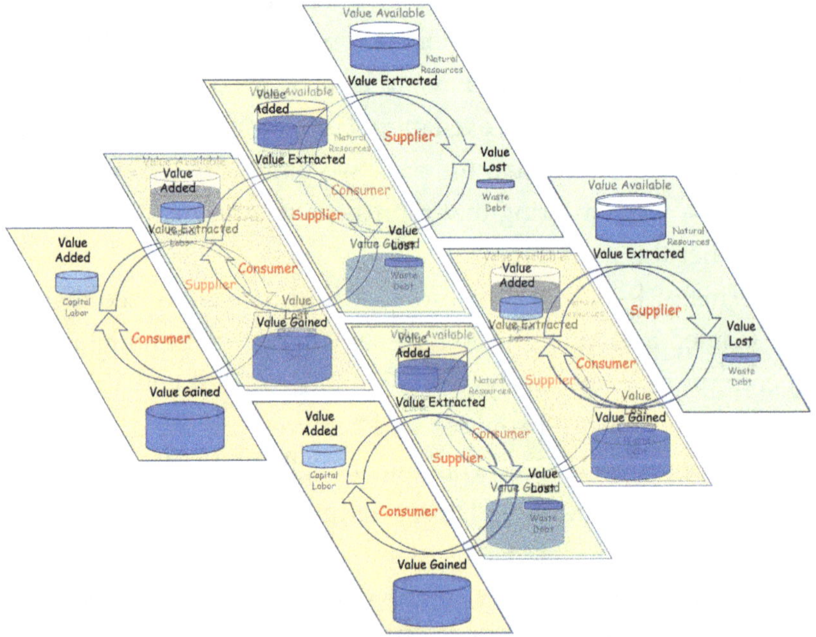

Figure 2.3. The overlapping cycles of value.

At this point, it is worth breaking down the connectivity of the various cycles of value in Figure 2.3 to see how they can relate to each other. Figure 2.4 displays all the possible positions that could be observed except for the cycles above Value Extracted and below the

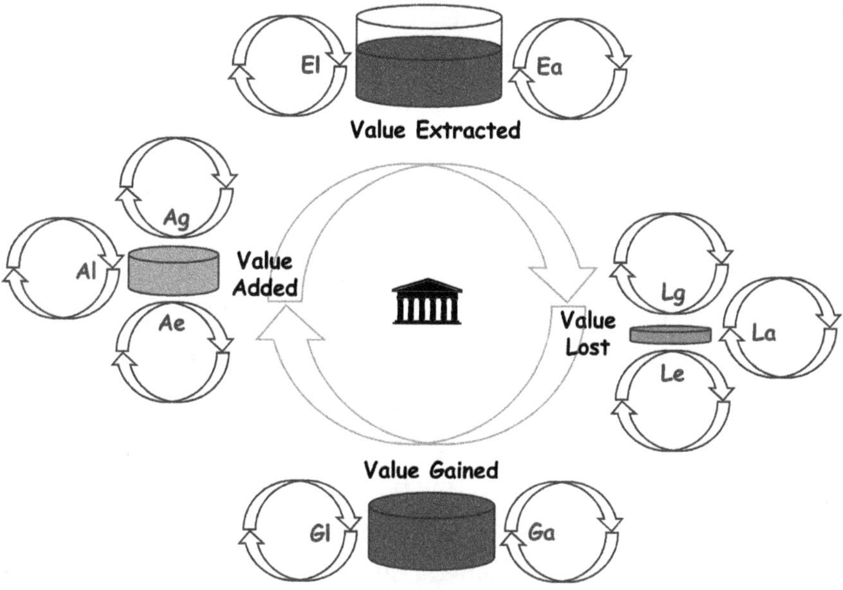

Figure 2.4.　The perspectives of value.

Value Gained, which are addressed separately through a producer–consumer interaction. Starting with the Value Extracted that has been seen at the top of the cycle, we need to see how it could serve as Value Added for someone else (Ea – the acronym means Value Extracted that is Value Added for someone else), while for another it can be seen as Value Lost (El). Consider the situation where we want to buy stocks of a company. Our Value Added here (Ea), among others, is the money we will spend to cover the cost of the stock. For the people who own that stock, the amount we spent represents their Value Extracted (Ea). In another scenario, we might have used borrowed money for the transaction. When we sell our stock, part of that money will be lost (El) to pay back the loan. In this case, our payback becomes the Value Extracted (El) for the bank that gave us the loan.

In the Value Gained case (bottom of Figure 2.4), we have two possibilities: to serve as Value Added (Ga) for someone else and Value Lost (Gl) for another. Following the stock scenario from before, if I were the broker mediating the transaction between the seller and buyer, I would then consider as my Value Gained part of the Value

Added (Ga) the buyer negotiated with the seller which I receive as my commission. Some of the Value Lost in the transaction of the stocks will go toward commissions to the exchange, making it in this way its Value Gained (Gl).

For the cases of the Values Added and Lost (Figure 2.4, left and right), we have three possibilities. For both, their value for someone else can be seen as Value Extracted, Value Gained, and Value Lost or Added, respectively. For example (Figure 2.5(a)), if we pay someone to do some work for us, then for that person our Value Added becomes their Value Extracted (Ae). If we used the money from a successful stock short, then that money (our Valued Added) is someone else's Value Lost (Al) (the person who invested in the stock going up). If we pay someone for a service, then part of our Value Added will be their Value Gained (Ag).

Similarly (Figure 2.5(b)), some of our Value Lost could be Value Gained (Lg) for the government as taxes for our transactions and it could be Value Extracted for someone who recycles our waste. Finally, loan interests are losses to us, but for the bank that collects them, they can be Value Added (La) toward further loans. The government can also use our Value Lost to provide better services to its citizens, so in that case, this amount of value will become Value Added toward those services.

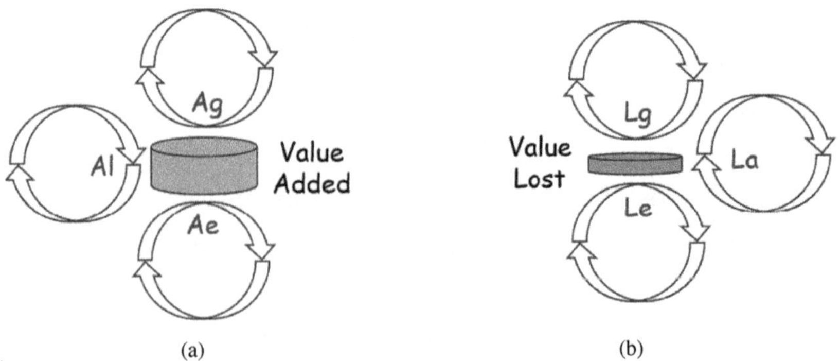

Figure 2.5.   Conversion of (a) Value Added and (b) Lost.

2.1 Producer and Consumer

With respect to the cycle of value from the market perspective, we need to consider multiple entities or agents as an interacting closed group. In its simplest form, that would include a two-member group engaged in a transaction. For the purposes of our discussion here, we consider one as the producer of a product or service and the other as its consumer. Figure 2.6 depicts the cycle of value considering the producer and consumer as two entities or agents that form a system. Both the producer and the consumer invest some Value Added to access the pool of Value Extracted and, in the process, lose some Value Lost. What the image does not show is the time frame of the transaction and what each of the entities considers as Value Extracted.

An alternative representation can be seen in Figure 2.7(a) where the producer–consumer system has been broken down into two separate cycles of value. We can see there that the consumer extracts

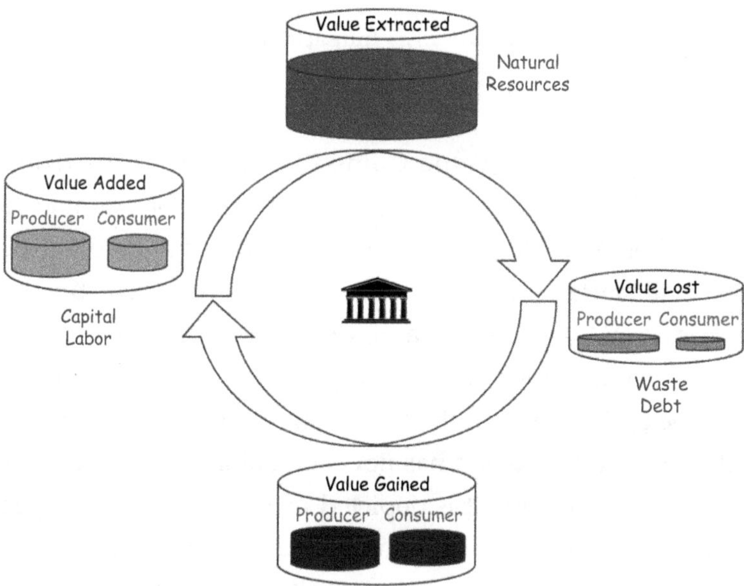

Figure 2.6.   Producer–consumer system.

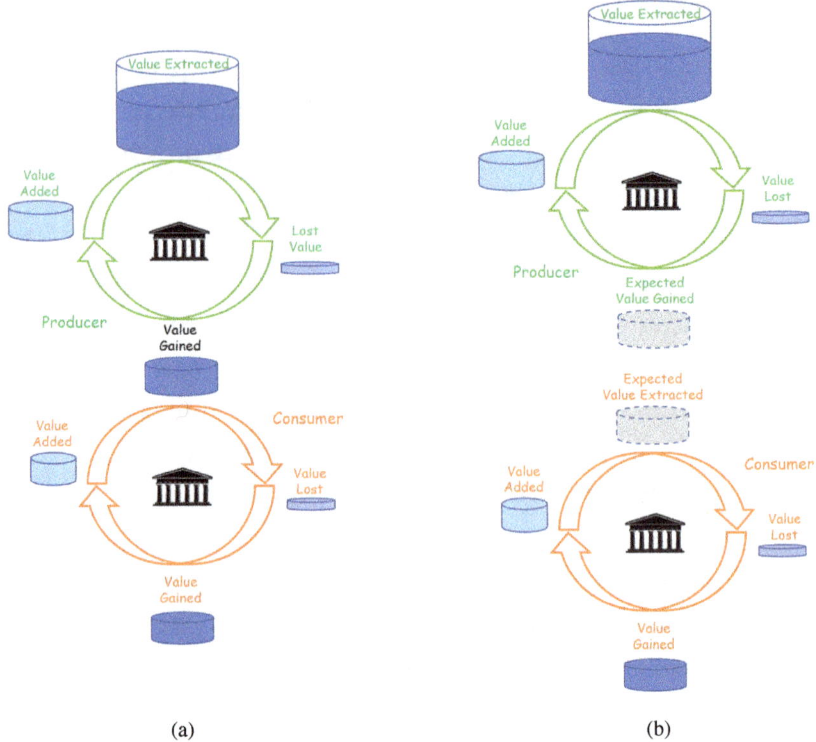

Figure 2.7.   Transaction.

value from the pool of Value Gained by the producer who has already gone through its own cycle of collecting it, for example, from nature, as their Value Extracted. Figure 2.7(b) expands the process in time. It all starts with the producer (green cycle) investing some Value Added (VA_p) to access Value Extracted (VE_p) from nature. In the process, some value (VL_p) is lost (production cost, energy losses, etc.) and the cycle ends with the Value Gained (VG_p) for the producer. Since the final Value Gained has not been gained yet (the consumer hasn't bought it already), it is depicted in Figure 2.7(b) as Expected Value Gained (VG_x) – the value the producer expects to gain. If the producer was operating in isolation $VG_x = VG_p$ but because the cycles are intertwined, we assume them to be different for now.

The process continues with the consumer now adding value (money, effort, etc.) (VA_c) to access what they believe can be extracted as Expected Value Extracted (VE_x). They also lose some value (VL_c) in the process (they might have to pay tax, spend time and effort, etc.) and eventually end with Value Gained (VG_c). Here too, if the cycle was operating in isolation, $VE_x = VE_c$, where VE_x would be the Value Extracted for the consumer.

Considering the cycle of value for producer and consumer (Figure 2.7(b)), we get

$$VA_p + VE_p = VL_p + VG_x$$

and

$$VA_c + VE_x = VL_c + VG_c$$

By adding the two equations, we get the cycle of value for the system producer–consumer:

$$VA_p + VA_c + VE_p + VE_x = VL_p + VL_c + VG_x + VG_c$$

When both producer and consumer have a perfect understanding of what they add and what they lose as well as what the producer extracts from nature and what the consumer gained at the end, then the only parts to be negotiated are VE_x and VG_x. The previous equation can then be written as

$$VE_x - VG_x = VL_p + VL_c + VG_c - VA_p - VA_c - VE_p$$

The right side of the equation can be considered constant or known (C) for the transaction, so the previous one becomes

$$VE_x - VG_x = C$$

It appears that what the consumer expects to extract minus what the producer expects to gain is some constant quantity C. In the case of $C = 0$, we have a perfect understanding between producer and consumer as

$$VE_x = VG_x$$

If $C > 0$, then $VE_x > VG_x$ which means the consumer extracts more value than what the producer gains. For the consumer, the cycles end up being a bargain even though he might not be aware of it. When $C < 0$, then $VE_x < VG_x$, and the producer gets the "bargain". The relationships reflect the typical operational environment of a transaction. Interestingly, if we were to consider marginal values, it will involve derivatives, and given that the derivative of the constant C is zero, we will have

$$VE_x' - VG_x' = 0$$

or

$$VE_x' = VG_x'$$

The rate (marginal) at which a consumer extracts value is the same as the rate (marginal) at which the producer gains value when the assumptions we considered are true.

To showcase what we've established up to here, let's consider a manufacturer that is producing a car and a consumer that buys the car to address his transportation needs. The manufacturer in his cycle contributes an initial value VA_p in the form of effort (including labor, machinery, tools, etc.) to access VE_p from nature (raw material). In the process, he will be losing value VL_p (inefficiencies, operational costs, etc.) and end up with gained value VG_p in the form of the car he produced. The law of conservation of value

$$VA_p + VE_p = VL_p + VG_p$$

in the form of specifics means

$$Effort + Nature = Inefficiencies + Car$$

The consumer now accesses the car as his extracted value VE_c by adding value VA_c as money or price. In the process, he experiences some losses VL_c, say taxes he had to pay, and ends up gaining value VG_c to satisfy his transportation needs. The law of conservation of value

$$VA_c + VE_c = VL_c + VG_c$$

in the form of specifics means

$$Price + Car = Taxes + Need$$

If we add the equations for the producer and consumer and eliminate the common term Car from the opposite sites of the equation, we get

$$Price + Effort + Nature = Taxes + Need + Inefficiencies$$

or

$$Price = Taxes + Need + Inefficiencies - Effort - Nature$$

We can see from the last equation that the price increases when Taxes are increased (naturally) or when the Need is high (demand or urgency or the function of the car) or when production Inefficiencies are high. The last one could be an indication that streamlining and automating manufacturing should be considered to reduce the price of the final product. The Effort has a negative sign suggesting that the less resources like labor, machinery, etc. you include the higher the price will be. Limited resources would naturally increase production time resulting in persisted Need which as we just mentioned will result in an increase in price. Similarly, scarcity of raw materials which reduces the contribution of the Nature term the result will be an increased price because the supply will not be enough to satisfy the demand.

The implications for policy formulation and decision-making should be abundant from the syllogisms that come from the combinations of the law of conservation of value in this simple case of the car manufacturer and the consumer. A government can control prices by reducing taxes, expanding public transportation to reduce the need for private means or cars, and supporting innovation initiatives and technology transfer to reduce inefficiencies in manufacturing. The individual manufacturer and the industry at large could invest more on labor upskilling and modernization of equipment and processes while also ensuring efficiencies of scale in retrieving raw material from nature. Multiple other examples could showcase the importance of the law of conservation of value for various stakeholders as it can help address multiple aspects of economic activity.

Considering marginal values (rates of changes), we just need to differentiate the last equation:

$$(\text{Price})' = (\text{Taxes})' + (\text{Need})' + (\text{Inefficiencies})' - (\text{Effort})' - (\text{Nature})'$$

Here, everything is a matter of how fast things change. Considering a small interval like say a month, one could assume that Taxes, Inefficiencies, Effort, and Nature remain constant and so their marginal values will be zero. In this case,

$$(Price)' = (Need)'$$

which is closer to the supply and demand concepts often used in simple economic calculations. The rate of change of the demand (in cars here) "causes" an equal rate of change in their price. The more cars are needed, the higher their price – all other factors being constant.

What we have discussed up to now with respect to the producer and consumer covers ideal situations that are valid only when the assumptions we made hold. A concept that directly relates to equilibrium in traditional economics is supply and demand. This is about the trade-off between the quantity produced that eventually reaches equilibrium when the quantity demanded equals the quantity produced. The cycle of value that is presented in this book is in essence a revival of the concept of supply and demand but with value instead of quantity and price.

There are two typical scenarios here that concern surplus or overproduction (Figure 2.8(a)) or shortage or underproduction (Figure 2.8(b)) on the part of the producer. In the case of surplus, we have overproduction because the actual demand VE is low, which means the producer has added more value VA that in essence is spilled or wasted, so it counts as lost value. In the cycle of value, this quantity will appear in the lost value and will eventually after the cycle returned to the producer. In the case of shortage, we have underproduction as there is available value for extraction VE, but the added value VA is not sufficient to extract it. This is a missed opportunity case and unextracted value (Value Spilled) will also have been accounted as loss that is returned back to the market. The cycle of value still applies, but the Value Spilled (VS) needs to be accounted for in the equations separately or integrated into the Value Lost.

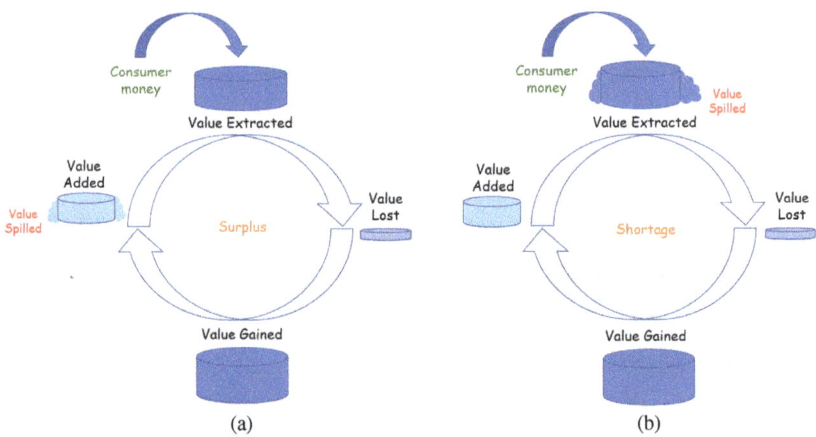

Figure 2.8. (a) Supply and (b) demand from the producer's perspective.

In real life, we will have repeated cycles as the market evolves in time. As the demand of a product or service increases, suppliers or producers will tend to produce more to make more profit. The increased quantities though will satisfy the demand or consumption, forcing the sellers to reduce the price to attract new buyers. We have in essence two opposing forces. Something like going to a restaurant when hungry. In the beginning, we are hungry and willing to pay a lot for the first bites of food, leading the owner to cook more to make us happy and earn money from us. The more we eat, the less hungry we become and the less willing we will be to pay as much as the first bites, so the owner will begin to reduce the price he is charging us for the remainder of the meal. At the same time, the supplier or producer needs to reduce the production of food because the market or we can't consume or eat anymore what is available. The cycle could repeat again with the same or a different product (for example, dessert).

2.2 The Market as a Closed System

We now take the producer–consumer model we developed and expand it to include multiple producers and consumers (Figure 2.9). We can easily assume each of the "buckets" in the cycle of value

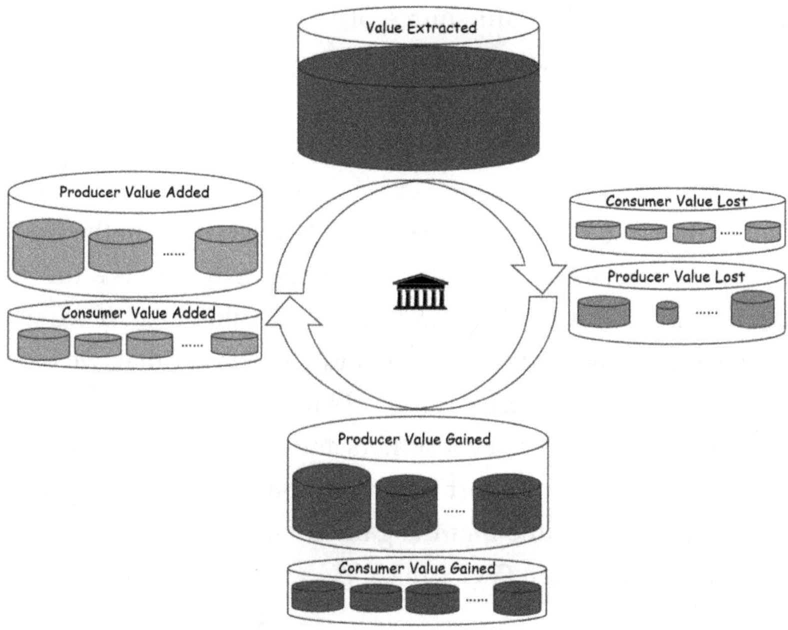

Figure 2.9. The market.

decomposed into multiple entities. We will call the producers P1, P2, …, Pn and the consumers C1, C2, …, Cm. The total number of producers and consumers can be different as one producer can be involved in cycles with multiple consumers and one consumer can be buying from different producers.

In the case of multiple actors in a market environment, the cycle of value will take the form (the index M is for market):

$$VA_M + VE_M = VL_M + VG_M$$

Each term in this equation is the sum of the corresponding terms of the participating entities. If we are interested in marginal values, then by differentiating the previous, we get

$$VA_M{}' + VE_M{}' = VL_M{}' + VG_M{}'$$

Assuming an abundant source of value for extraction, as it is typically assumed of nature ($VE_M' = 0$), we get

$$VG_M' = VA_M' - VL_M'$$

This result suggests that the Marginal Value Gained in the market (which can be seen as a proxy for market growth rate) is a function of the Marginal Value Added and Marginal Value Lost. If we want the market to grow, then we need to add value faster than we lose it.

Another interesting result can be obtained if we consider a fixed market size (the number of consumers and producers is constant – a realistic assumption for short time periods) and a certain stability, then we can also assume that the gained value does not change or it can reach a maximum ($VG = \max$, $VG_M' = 0$) past which it cannot grow. At that point,

$$VA_M' = VL_M'$$

For a stable market, we need to match the speed at which we lose value with the speed we add value.

Balancing the cycles of value of the various transactions to adhere to the law of conservation of value can be challenging due to the multiplicity of the involved entities. It becomes difficult to realistically model agents with different experiences, priorities, and goals. Representing reality is very difficult (see Section 4.5) as we rarely know exactly what the Value Extracted is, how much we need to add to get it, how much we will lose in the process, and how much we will eventually gain. There is an inherent uncertainty in every term of equation (1.1) that we will represent here as error terms. We will have error terms for Value Added (VA_{error}), Value Extracted (VE_{error}), Value Lost (VL_{error}), and Value Gained (VG_{error}). The error quantities here are assumed to have the error sign included in them.

Considering the error terms, the law of conservation of value for one cycle will become

$$(VA + VA_{error}) + (VE + VE_{error}) = (VG + VG_{error}) + (VL + VL_{error})$$

It should be apparent from the assumption we made in the cases we have seen so far that there are multiple sources of error that should be accounted for. While this is true for the single case cycle, it is less of an issue for the total or market case where multiple entities participate in different cycles. In that case, the previous equation would be the sum of all individual cycles that take part over a period of time:

$$\sum (VA + VA_{error}) + \sum (VE + VE_{error})$$
$$= \sum (VG + VG_{error}) + \sum (VL + VL_{error})$$

or

$$\sum VA + \sum VA_{error} + \sum VE + \sum VE_{error}$$
$$= \sum VG + \sum VG_{error} + \sum VL + \sum VL_{error}$$

The law of large populations will ensure that in the general case, we will have as many deviations up as we have down and in this way, the sums of the error terms will tend to diminish. In statistical terminology, we can say that as long as the sphericity is low, and the deviations from the mean are random (do not follow a pattern), equation (1.1) holds as representative of multiple cycles of value like a whole market:

$$\sum VA + \sum VE = \sum VG + \sum VL$$

The summation symbol will be assumed in all expressions of value from now on when we talk about the market and the economy in general.

3

ECONOMY AND GOVERNMENT

So far, we discussed the cycle of value as a single isolated process or a group of processes that form a market. Expanding the concept to the economy at large, we can imagine each entity or agent in the economy going through its own cycles of value at each moment in time while interacting with each other and with nature (Figure 3.1). Nature can be considered a passive agent in this scenario that only provides value (at least while it lasts). An agent X might want to access the VE value of another agent Y or nature. That could happen when, for example, X pays Y (VA) to do some work (VE), the result of which is VG for X. In the process, some value will be lost to the environment (VL) either as waste, taxes, insurance payments, or something else. The situation could involve organizations or even whole countries when they interact with other organizations or countries. Each entity in the cycle of value of Figure 3.1 is represented by a different shape container. We discuss in more detail this aspect of the participating entities in Chapter 4 when we consider value as needed. The government and/or international institutions play the role of coordinator or controller in this situation.

A source of value can be accessed by multiple agents that could either compete or cooperate in the process. Financial institutions can reliably be described in cycles of value. A bank could borrow money from a central bank as VG for its purposes. It could then lend that money (VG) to other banks, organizations, and individuals. In this case, the VG of the lending bank will play the role of VE for the

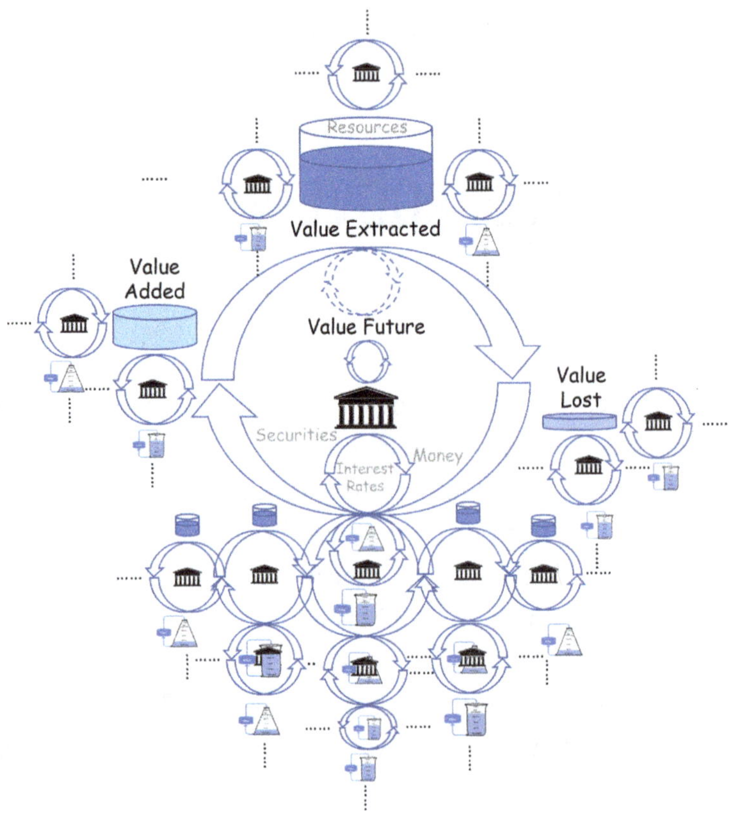

Figure 3.1. The economy at the level of a country.

borrowing entities. In return, the bank gains value from the lending process through the interest it charges, while in the process it loses some value as it has to pay for its facilities, employees, etc. and also return some money with interest to the central bank.

There is a little "magic" going on in this case as one might wonder what or where the source of the value the government or federal reserve or central bank accesses is. The word "magic" is not really used metaphorically here as the government can literally print paper out of thin air that it will "baptize" as a value called *money*. As we see later in this chapter, the logic behind this is to "borrow" money from the future and return it (burn the paper money really) when the future becomes present.

Apart from influencing the flow of value by creating the imaginary VE source called money, the government can also access the VE containers of the entities in its jurisdiction by setting and collecting value from them as taxes, fines, etc. under the pretext of services rendered. Such services include but are not limited to supporting security forces that ensure the physical independence and safety of a territory, by providing healthcare and educational services, etc. Through trade deals, the government can also access or borrow from the VE pools that other entities like organizations, individuals, and other countries form. It can even work collaboratively with other governments to access natural pools and even whole countries through occupations. Space exploration is an example of collaboration among countries to access the potential value they predict it represents.

While references to government have been made in previous sections, a more in-depth discussion in light of the cycle of value is required to shed light on its function and role in the economy. For the purposes of this analysis, we view economies as systems of entities that interact or transact in a natural or geographic setting. Such systems interact with other systems physically and virtually through an exchange of inputs and outputs. These could be in the form of resources, products, services, labor, and currency transferred between economies. The role of government in this respect is double. The primary role is that of the controller and coordinator of economic activity, while the secondary is that of an entity within the economy that aims to sustain itself. So, government can be seen both as external to the economy and also as internal and an integral part of it.

3.1   Government as Controller

A core ingredient of the cycle of value for the economy is the control mechanisms that are needed to ensure its continuous flow. Here is where the government plays its critical role. Inefficiencies in the cycle (like economic downtimes) can be addressed by decreasing interest rates at the federal government level, by printing money, or by establishing laws and regulations to support economic growth. The question is as follows: What is the government's source of value that it would "generously" allow organizations and individuals to access? In the past, governments would accumulate gold whose value was perceived as timeless. It would then print money as a proxy to gold and allow its constituents access to them in the form of loans. These loans would be directly available to the banking system that served as the intermediary between the government and organizations or citizens. The money would be invested to produce more wealth than what was borrowed, allowing organizations and individuals to repay the banks and keep the remaining as profit.

The banks would then pay back the government the money they borrowed plus interest and keep the remaining as their profit. As a result of economic activity, the government would increase its money deposits through taxes after subtracting the costs of sustaining its operations (Figure 3.2). This extra amount of money could then be invested in services to its citizens and maybe purchasing more gold. The process is straightforward enough to the point of the United States (US) government realizing that they really did not need the gold in the cycle, so they just decided to do away with it altogether. From that point on, the US government just printed money any time it was needed to stimulate the economy and withdrew money to slow it down. The rationale for eliminating gold from the cycle was the sheer faith that the US brand was enough to ensure the cycle will keep going forever. Money will be printed at some point in time and be returned at a future point in time. In this way, the "future" becomes the source of value.

Figure 3.3 shows how the money the government prints circulates in the economy. The figure depicts the cycle of value for an organization (or individual) that borrows from a bank (red icon). The money is invested along with other capital and labor in the form of added value to extract value from natural resources

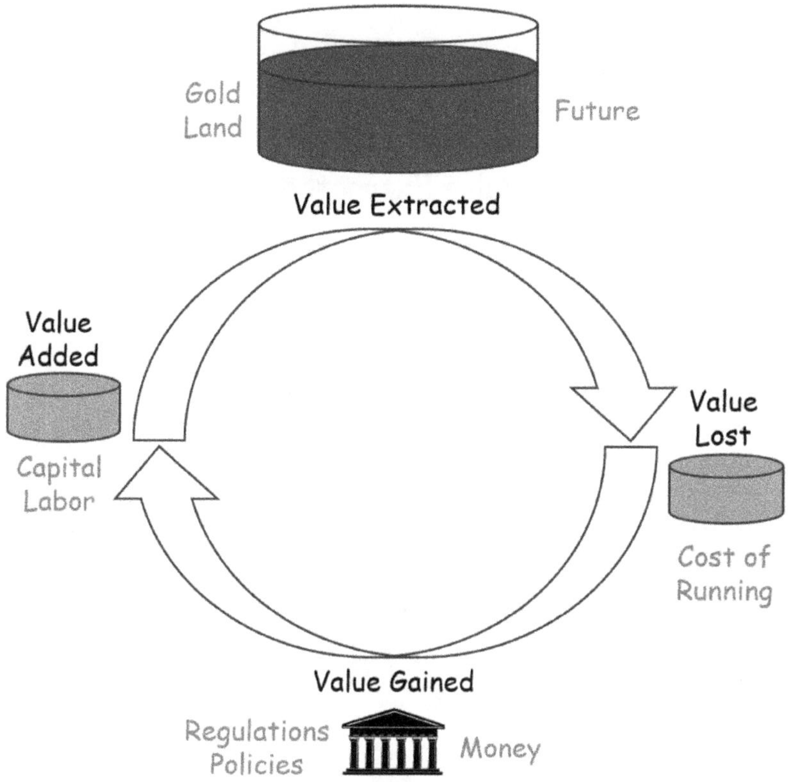

Figure 3.2. The government cycle of value.

in this case. In the process, some value is lost, and the residual value, following the law of conservation of value, becomes the VG for the organization. This value can later be extracted by other organizations or individuals as it becomes accessible or consumed for organizational functions.

The bank acquired its VE from the central bank (black icon) by selling securities or debt in exchange for money. The role of the central bank as representative of the government and by extension the people was simply to access future value (a promise really) and convert it into money (VG for the central bank) by adding value through capital and labor required for its operations (mainly the cost of printing the money). To account for its losses, the central bank will

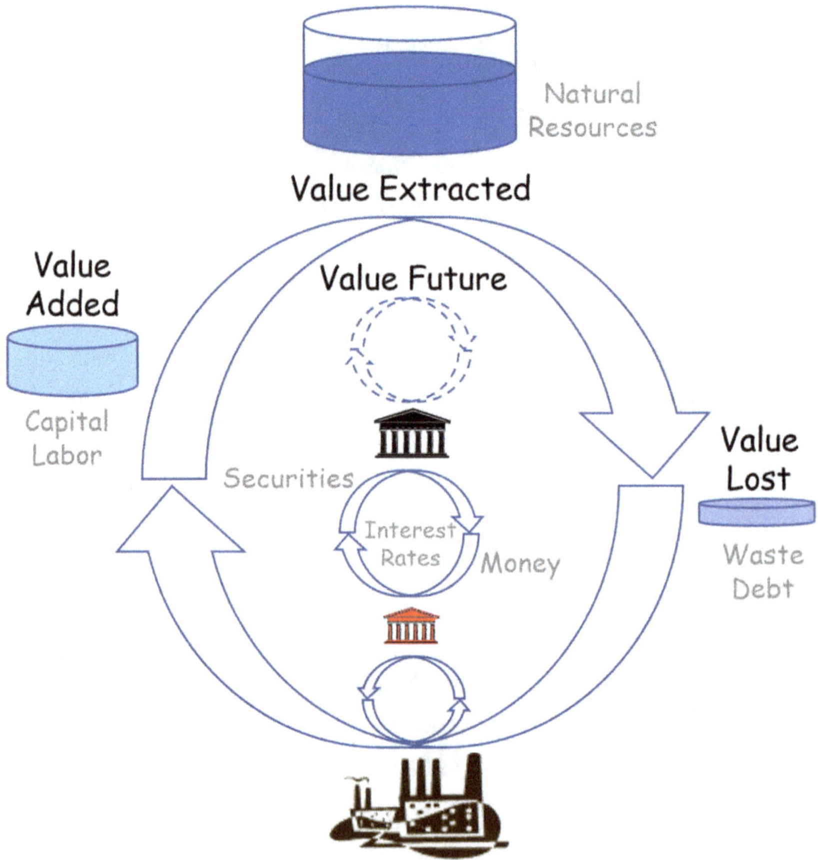

Figure 3.3. The flow of value with government as controller.

receive funds from the government and will gain interest when the banks repay their loans.

For the cycle to work properly, uncertainties need to be addressed or at least considered in real time. The whole system is based on the trust that all entities will pay back their dues when the time comes. This is not what always happens, especially in cases of economic uncertainties when banks overextend their "trust" lending money they are not getting back when businesses go bankrupt. As a result, banks can go bust and be unable to fulfill their commitment to return the money they took from the central bank or government.

The government experiences a shortage in its balance sheet that it typically covers by drawing more from the future (printing more money) or borrowing from other governments and/or individuals (like by issuing bonds). The purpose of the government as controller and coordinator is to stabilize prices, moderate long-term interest rates, reduce unemployment, and in general sustain the economy through cycles of value.

A case might help highlight the previous discussion. Let us apply the cycle of value in the case of the government subsidizing an industry such as the shale oil and gas industry by making available low interest rates to them. The tipping balance in Figure 3.4 shows the effect of lowering interest rates (red arrow in Figure 3.4).

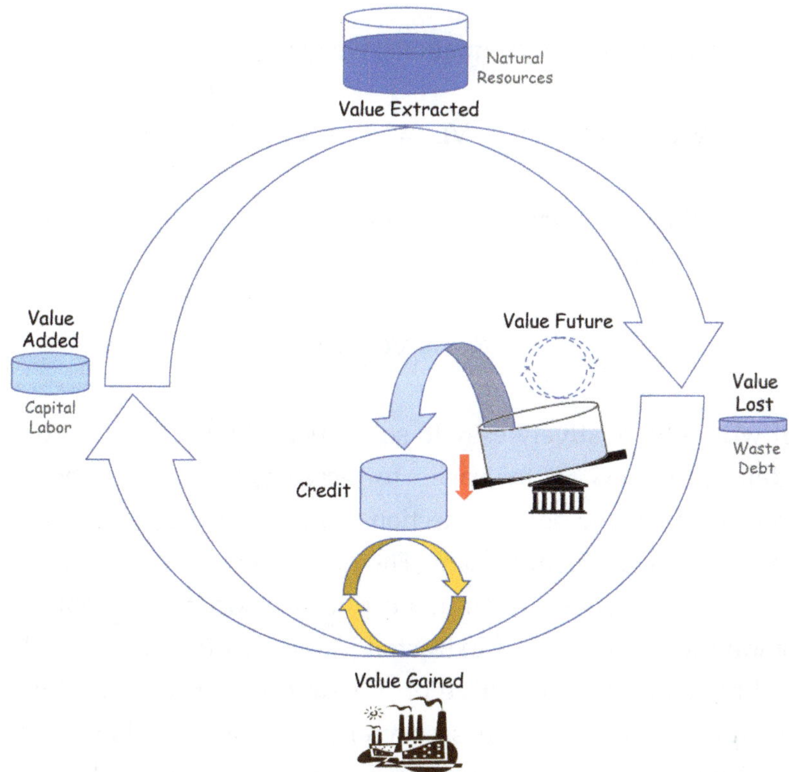

Figure 3.4. Cycles of value for shale oil and gas companies.

Let us now apply the cycle of value for the organization and the two pools of value it can access: the natural and the government-created credit. For the former (outer cycle in Figure 3.4), we assign the index "n" to indicate the "natural" cycle or the one that accesses natural resources. We have

$$VA_n + VE_n = VL_n + VG_n$$

For the internal cycle (orange colored in Figure 3.4 and expanded in Figure 3.5), we assign the index "g" to indicate the government-supported (banking sector) cycle (Figure 3.5). We have

$$VA_g + VE_g = VL_g + VG_g$$

By adding the last two equations, we get

$$VA_n + VA_g + VE_n + VE_g = VL_n + VL_g + VG_n + VG_g$$

The goal of the organization would presumably be to maximize $VG_n + VG_g$. This can be achieved when

$$VG_n' + VG_g' = 0$$

It would be relatively easy to see, especially based on historical evidence, that VG_g' is far easier to increase, especially when the organization has the right connections that can ensure loans from the banking or government system. The question would be as follows: Why would the government in a capitalistic society ever bother to provide the credit pool of Extracted Value for organizations? This could be a strategic objective of the government to stimulate or make it attractive for businesses to engage in a cycle that accesses special types of natural resources, for example, renewable energy

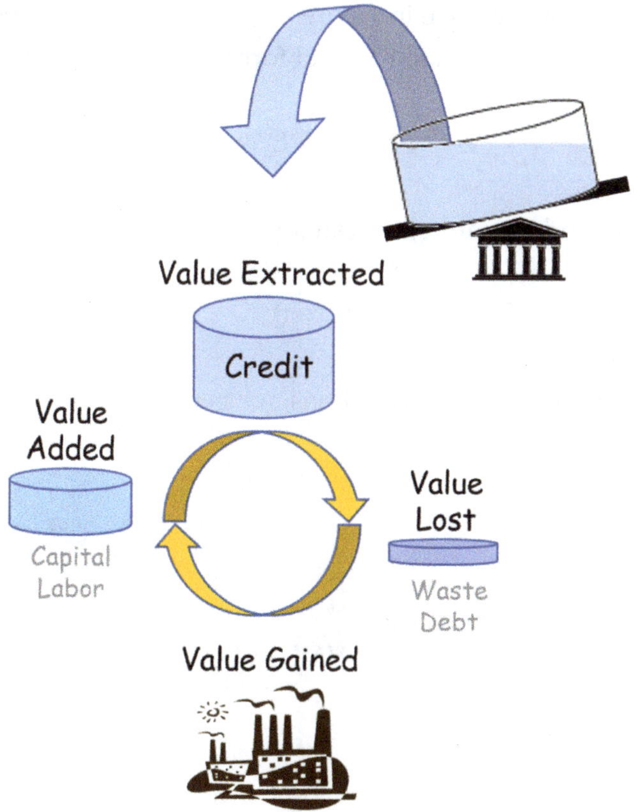

Figure 3.5. Government-subsidized cycles of value.

sources. The downside is that if this process continues, then you have an industry highly dependent on government subsidies as the easier route to sustain their growth than investing in innovating to optimize production and distribution.

From the government's point of view, the question is when it should pull out the extra pool of value that it made available. The typical answer here is when the industry can sufficiently sustain itself through the natural cycle. Considering the available natural resources as constant or at least accessible at a constant rate (the average availability of wind or sunlight won't change), then for the nature cycle (outside cycle in Figure 3.4), we can consider the law of conservation of value in its marginal form:

$$VA_n' + VE_n' = VL_n' + VG_n'$$

For an abundant nature, we can assume

$$VE_n' = 0 \tag{3.1}$$

Combining the last two equations, we get

$$VA_n' = VL_n' + VG_n'$$

or

$$VG_n' = VA_n' - VL_n'$$

For $VG_n' > 0$, we get

$$VA_n' > VL_n'$$

This means that gains will keep accumulating as long as the Marginal Value Added is higher than the Marginal Value Lost (all other influencing factors excluded). In the limit, the two sides of the inequality will be equal:

$$VA_n' = VL_n' \tag{3.2}$$

For the government-supported cycle now (Figure 3.5), the marginal form of the law of conservation of value will take the form

$$VA_g' + VE_g' = VL_g' + VG_g'$$

$$\text{or}$$

$$VE_g' = VL_g' + VG_g' - VA_g'$$

If we consider the government's point of view here, then

$$VE_g' < 0$$

In other words, the government would want to decrease the amount of subsidizing available to the industry. In that case, the last two equations give

$$VL_g' + VG_g' - VA_g' < 0$$

$$\text{or}$$

$$VL_g' + VG_g' < VA_g'$$

Considering the limit when the inequality becomes equality, we get

$$VL_g' + VG_g' = VA_g' \tag{3.3}$$

Let us now consider the marginal form of the law of conservation of value for both cycles:

$$VA_n' + VA_g' + VE_n' + VE_g' = VL_n' + VL_g' + VG_n' + VG_g'$$

Applying (3.1), we get

$$VA_n' + VA_g' + VE_g' = VL_n' + VL_g' + VG_n' + VG_g'$$

Applying (3.2), we get

$$VA_g' + VE_g' = VL_g' + VG_n' + VG_g'$$

Applying (3.3), we get

$$VE_g' = VG_n'$$

In other words, the government should start reducing the subsidies when the rate of the credit it provides is equal to the rate of gain the industry makes from the natural cycle. Past that point, the government has no reason to keep supporting an industry. Having said that, if the industry is critical to the survival of its citizens, the government should revert to other means of supporting the industry, including the option of nationalizing it as it does with security and healthcare services.

Another interesting application of the law of conservation of value for the government is in relation to unemployment and inflation. Let us consider the cycle of value as representing the economy at some point t in time:

$$VA_t + VE_t = VL_t + VG_t$$

or

$$VG_t = VA_t + VE_t - VL_t$$

Let us consider that a government through various measures (government magic) is reducing unemployment or increasing wages. This will allow more purchasing power to enter the economy. In the cycle of value, this will appear as added value VA_{t+1} due to the additional purchasing power of the unemployed who got jobs and receive salaries (presumably higher than the unemployment benefits). In this case, we will have

$$VA_{t+1} + VE_{t+1} = VL_{t+1} + VG_{t+1}$$

or

$$VG_{t+1} = VA_{t+1} + VE_{t+1} - VL_{t+1}$$

By subtracting the equations for $t + 1$ and t, we get

$$VG_{t+1} - VG_t = VA_{t+1} - VA_t + VE_{t+1} - VE_t - VL_{t+1} + VL_t$$

Considering the economy doesn't gain anything from the move and nothing additional is lost,

$$VG_{t+1} = VG_t \qquad \text{and} \qquad VL_{t+1} = VL_t$$

so our equation will become

$$VA_{t+1} - VA_t + VE_{t+1} - VE_t = 0$$

If we view the previous as differences, we get

$$\Delta VA_{t+1} + \Delta VE_t = 0$$

or

$$\Delta VA_{t+1} = -\Delta VE_t$$

This means the positive increase in the added value due to the influx of job income will result in a decrease in the value extracted. Otherwise, the same amount of money will buy you less than it did before. Thus, we have the onset of inflation where the surplus of purchasing power is balanced by inflation. For the cycle to balance out ($VG_{t+1} = VG_t$) or produce sustainable growth ($VG_{t+1} > VG_t$) with low or zero unemployment and steady market prices, either the extracted value or the lost value or a combination of the two must be increased. Increasing the extracted value can happen through innovation or by extracting more from the environment, while increasing the lost value can happen with increased taxation. The former is ideal, while the latter is bound to create some societal unrest. A worst-case scenario is if economic uncertainty guides consumers to reserve their money in savings.

The Philips curve in policy formulation can be derived from the law of conservation of value by applying the previous logic. Let us consider the added value in the cycle as the influx of money due to the unemployment that got employed as U and the lost value as u (remember the linear expression of the law at the end of Section 1.1). Assuming an inflation rate of π and β_1, the amount of unemployment (in money influx terms) that causes inflation to rise by 1 unit, we can express our extracted value as $\pi \times \beta_1$. If the aim was to stabilize the economy, then the gained value due to the whole process is β_0 and the law of conservation of value

$$VA + VE = VL + VG$$

becomes

$$U + \pi \times \beta_1 = \beta_0 + u$$

or

$$U = \beta_0 - \pi \times \beta_1 + u$$

which is the classic form of the Phillips curve. During the 1960s, this equation (with $u = 0$) was a guiding framework for understanding the relationship between unemployment and inflation. The U.S. economy displayed the classic Phillips curve trade-off, where efforts to reduce unemployment were accompanied by rising inflation. This inverse relationship led policymakers to believe that they could manage the economy by adjusting inflation and unemployment through monetary and fiscal measures. One can only imagine how far off from reality such implementation can be if we just consider the assumptions made like zero innovation capabilities and a steady rate of extracting value from the environment. Additionally, ignoring the lost value is of major concern as it can be an important factor in formulating policy that would stabilize the cycle of value.

3.2   Government as Organization

In this section, we see value from the perspective of the government as an independent or "selfish" organization. The challenge here is the dual role the government plays as it is both the recipient and provider of value. While the value creation part has been discussed to some extent in the previous section, we see the government here as a consumer of value. As such, the value pool it can access includes the economy and natural resources (Figure 3.6). In terms of the economy, the government can access the wealth of its citizens and the organizations within its jurisdiction through various forms of taxation (income taxes, insurance contributions, etc.) and returns on investments (interests on loans, stocks in businesses, etc.) as well as by accessing the global market such as by borrowing from other countries and institutions. In terms of natural resources, this is typically done by its proxies that could include nationalized organizations, institutes (academic, research, etc.), and subsidies. Finally, another resource the government can access is the goodwill and compliance of its citizens.

In terms of the cycle of value, the government can access the aforementioned pools by adding value in the form of establishing policies, laws, and mechanisms for their enforcement, as well as by providing services citizens need, such as healthcare, security, education, etc. In the process, the government will lose value in the form of cost for running its operations (public sector) and fulfilling its obligations to its internal and external stakeholders (for example,

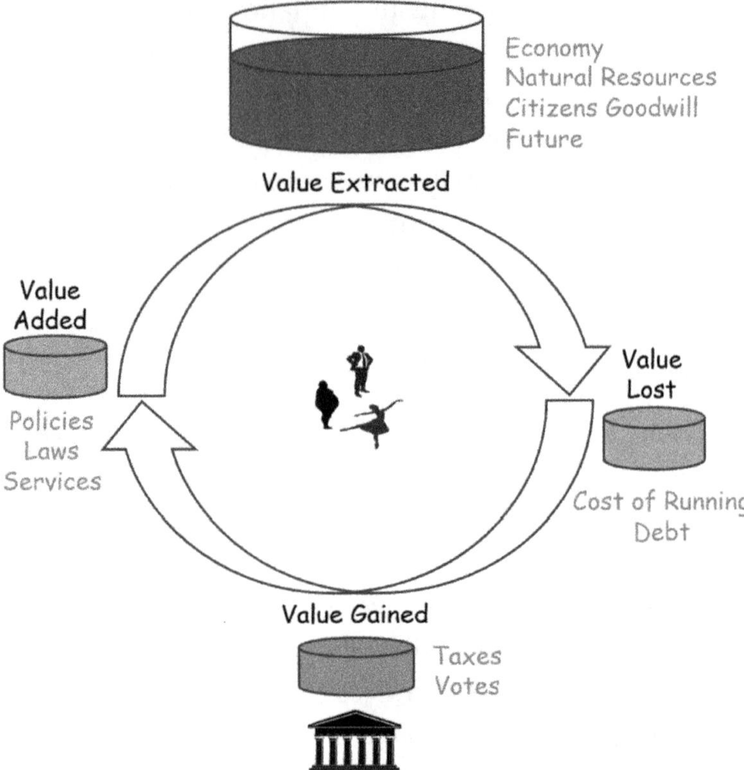

Figure 3.6.   Government as an organization.

paying debt). Eventually, the government will gain value in the form of taxes and income from its subsidies as well as in the form of confidence or votes of its citizens. The role of the ultimate controller, in the case of democratically elected governments, is the voting population.

While the cycle of value for the government is no different from any other value cycle, it is worth describing the high-level internals of the cycle. One such possibility is presented in Figure 3.7 where the cycle is decoupled into two interconnected cycles. When a political party is elected, it forms a government. For simplicity, here, we assume the political party got a full majority and the government it formed is its proxy. So, the inner cycle (blue coloration) starts with the

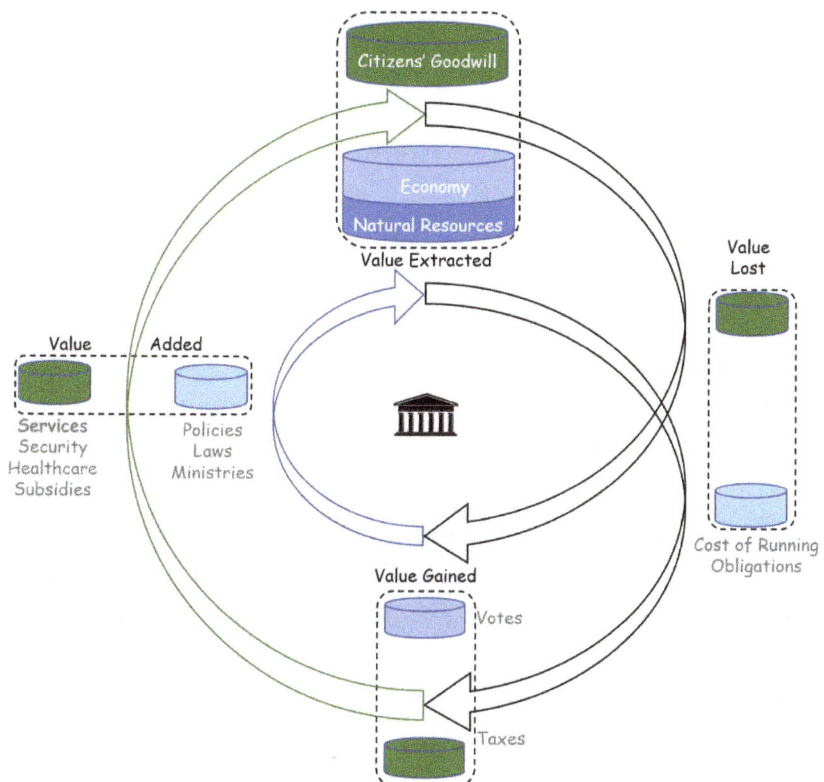

Figure 3.7. Interconnected cycles of value.

vote of confidence the government received. The government then exerts some effort by adding value (VA) through laws and policies enacted by its various ministries to access the pool of VE. This VE could be in the form of natural resources accessed by nationalized industries or through subsidies to businesses that access the natural resources on its behalf. One such example could be a nuclear power station the government operates, while another could be the financial support the government provides to the renewables industry to support a carbon-free economy. The VE for the government could also be the economy it controls as it can impose taxes or by selling or rending resources like land, securities, etc. In the process, the government is losing some value mainly due to running expenses, and obligations to its creditors and constituents. The result is VG (summarized as taxes in Figure 3.7).

This "inner" part of the value cycle can be expressed as (the lower-case index g indicates government)

$$VA_g + VE_g = VL_g + VG_g$$

In part or in total, the value the government gained up to now is encapsulated for convenience as taxes and goes toward services it provides to its citizens (outside cycle with green coloration in Figure 3.7). This can be seen as the VA the government contributes to access the goodwill of its citizens (playing the role of VE). Again, some value will be lost, typically as the cost for supporting the public sector. In return, the government gains the confidence of its citizens translated as votes at election time and support in-between (such as, say, no strikes).

This "outer" part of the value cycle can be expressed as (the lower-case index c indicates citizens)

$$VA_c + VE_c = VL_c + VG_c$$

Adding the equations of the two cycles, we get

$$VA_g + VA_c + VE_g + VE_c = VL_g + VL_c + VG_g + VG_c$$

Considering marginal components or differentiating the previous equation, we get

$$VA_g' + VA_c' + VE_g' + VE_c' = VL_g' + VL_c' + VG_g' + VG_c' \qquad (3.4)$$

At this point, we can investigate some potential scenarios. Considering the government as a "selfish" entity, it would want to maximize its VG. Maximizing a quantity means having its first derivative as zero. In this case, this means that

$$VG_g' + VG_c' = 0 \qquad \text{or} \qquad VG_g' = -VG_c' \qquad (3.5)$$

This means that the maximum gains for the government are achieved when the rate of change of taxes (margin of taxes) is opposite to the rate of change of votes or citizen confidence (all other factors excluded). The more taxes a government is imposing, the more negative value from votes it will receive. This is a profound reality that almost anyone will agree with. Nevertheless, it is a natural outcome of the analysis we performed.

Let us follow up this finding with the total cycle of value as expressed by equation (3.4) when considering equation (3.5):

$$(3.4) => VA_g' + VA_c' + VE_g' + VE_c' = VL_g' + VL_c' \qquad (3.6)$$

If we now decouple VE_g to a part that refers to natural resources VE_n and one that refers to the economy VE_e, we have

$$VE_g = VE_n + VE_e$$

and

$$VE_g' = VE_n' + VE_e'$$

Since nature is considered abundant, we have $VE_n' = 0$, so the previous equation becomes $VE_g' = VE_e'$.

If we also group the added and lost values as totals ($VA_g + VA_c = VA$ and $VL_g + VL_c = VL$), then (3.6) becomes

$$VA' + VE_e' + VE_c' = VL'$$

$$\text{or}$$

$$VE_e' + VE_c' = VL' - VA'$$

This equation was derived for the case where the government maximizes its gains. If at the same time the government wants to minimize its interference (VE = minimum), then $VE_e' + VE_c' = 0$, so

$$VL' - VA' = 0$$

$$\text{or}$$

$$VA' = VL'$$

All the government needs to do for an "idyllic" society is to keep the rate of value it adds equal to the rate of value it loses on average in the cycles of value it engages (same as equation 3.2).

The oxymoron with the government, especially when supported by absolute majority, is that it often functions as both an element of the economy and as its regulator. A separation of these roles in theory is realized by the independence of its executive, legislative, and judiciary branches. Ultimately, a democratic government regulates itself through the parliament, the judiciary, and self-regulation (redesign), except during election time when citizens decide its future.

4

EXPRESSIONS OF VALUE

At the beginning of this book, we considered the abstract concept of value as representing a "real" entity that can be exchanged between actors and pools or containers of it. In this chapter, we consider possible representatives of value and their combinations in an attempt to demonstrate the use of the cycle of value and the laws or expressions of value we derived. As such proxies of value such as capital, utility, revenue, information, and need will be considered. Energy is also a very popular proxy for value, so the following chapter is dedicated to discussing it further and more specifically by analogy to value than an actual substitute.

4.1   Value as Capital

As the first case in point, we assume that value represents only money. For example, consider depositing an X amount of money in a savings account that offers $r\%$ interest rate (compounded monthly), while a monthly maintenance fee of Y amount of money is applied. In the context of the cycle of value (assume one calendar year), it can be easily seen that at the end of the cycle or year,

$$VA = X$$

$$VE = rX$$

$$VL = 12Y$$

In order to calculate our gained value, we can apply the law of conservation of value:

$$VA + VE = VL + VG$$

or

$$VG = VA + VE - VL$$

or

$$VG = X + rX - 12Y$$

or

$$VG = X(r+1) - 12Y$$

For the second year, the previous amount (VG) will be our Value Added, so

$$VA = X(r+1) - 12Y$$
$$VE = r[X(r+1) - 12Y]$$
$$VL = 12Y$$

Applying again the law of conservation of value, we get

$$VG = X(r+1) - 12Y + r[X(r+1) - 12Y] - 12Y$$

or

$$VG = X(r+1) - 12Y + rX(r+1) - r12Y - 12Y$$

or

$$VG = X(r+1)(n+1) - 12Y(r + 2)$$
$$VG = X(r+1)2 - 12Y(r + 2)$$

It might be evident that as we keep compounding, the first term will be the classical compounding formula for principle X after a number of years t:

$$X[(r/12) + 1]^{12t}$$

while the second term will represent the losses.

4.2   Value as Utility

The concept of utility as applied today is fundamentally flawed as it ignores the reality of the market and the economy at large. The fallacy is that utility starts at a maximum and gradually diminishes. In that respect, this model ignores how that maximum is reached. Let's consider the example often cited in the literature and based on the notion that an agent's actions seek to increase pleasure and avoid pain. The unit typically assumed is that of "utils". Let's say I eat a banana and I get 8 utils or pleasure or satisfaction. The theory of marginal utility states that if I eat a second banana, the additional pleasure I will get will be less than the first, say 7 (total of utils 15). If we continue like this, the additional pleasure will be diminishing, say by 1 util each time, so after 6 more bananas, I will stop getting any more utils or pleasure. In fact, after 8 bananas, I should start feeling some discomfort, experiencing negative marginal utility. This will continue until death do us part (the bananas and I). Figure 4.1(a) depicts the neoclassical view that utility will be decreasing with quantity.

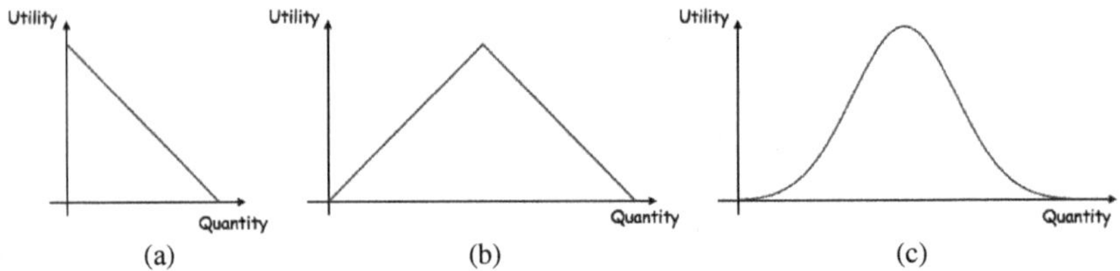

Figure 4.1. Utility functions.

Now, if instead of bananas I eat chocolate, the situation will be radically different for me. The first chocolate will give me say 10 utils but will make me crave for a second, so I would expect 11 more utils (total of 21). The third will probably follow the same pattern, say 12 more utils, and only after that will my marginal utility start falling. If the case of the chocolate seems extreme, consider being hungry, starving really, and someone offers you a grain of fried rice which to you represents, say, 1 util. Do you believe the next grain will offer you less pleasure? It should be evident in that case that your marginal utility will be going up with each grain of fried rice until you reach a saturation point past which you would expect your marginal utility to start going down. Figure 4.1(b) and Figure 4.2 display the more natural situation where utility is increased until a saturation point is reached and then it starts decreasing.

The linear function of utility that has been described up to now might not be as reflective of reality and one might experiment with other forms like the standardized normal distribution of Figure 4.1(c)

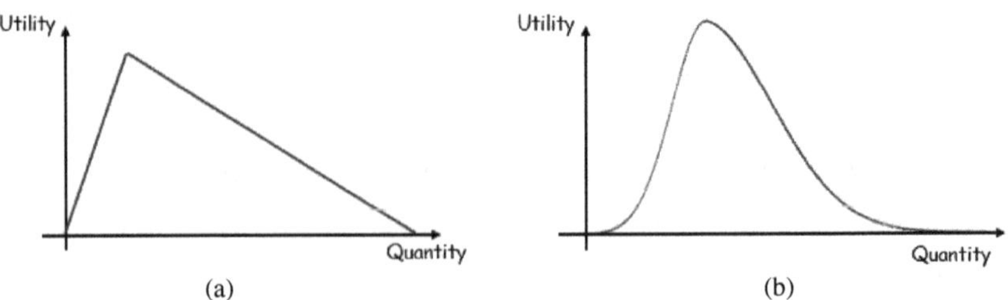

Figure 4.2. Utility functions with bias.

or the skewed forms of Figure 4.2. By equating value (V) with utility (U), the law of conservation of value will become

$$(1.1) => UA + UE = UL + UG$$

Everything we discussed in the previous chapters can be applied here with utility instead of value. In economics, utility U is often associated with consumption C, so it is typically expressed as $U(C)$. Since utility typically deteriorates over time (how much additional pleasure can one get by eating one more chocolate after eating 100), we expect it to deteriorate over time. Consumption in this way acts as a proxy for utility which in this example is equivalent to value.

As an example, let us assume that we add value through labor L that results in income I as extracted value. We consume an amount C as lost value and hopefully, we gain value as money M. According to the law of conservation of value, we will have

$$VA + VE = VL + VG$$

or

$$L + I = C + M$$

Assuming we used the minimum possible consumption, and the income was high due to our skills and experience, we managed to save a lot. We decide to invest the amount M in another cycle of value so this time it becomes our added value. Using the index t to indicate the time of the execution of the cycle and assuming a year as the period it took for the cycle to complete at the end of the year (presume we get paid yearly for simplicity), we will have

$$M + I_t = C_t + S_t$$

where I_t is the income at the end of the year, C_t is the amount we consumed throughout the year, and S_t is the amount of savings we end up with. Of course, if we consumed more than what was available, S_t will be negative representing borrowed money. For now, we will assume we were conservative, and S_t is positive representing saving. A typical assumption in economics is that you get paid from the beginning before, so you have money to sustain your consumption, so $M = 0$. The previous equation then becomes

$$I_t = C_t + S_t$$

or

$$S_t = I_t - C_t \tag{4.1}$$

If we consider another cycle/year as $(t + 1)$, then

$$(1+r)S_t + I_{t+1} = C_{t+1} + S_{t+1}$$

Economists, for simplicity, like to consider that $S_{t+1} = 0$ as if the $(t + 1)$ year is the last year of your life, so there is no real point in having savings for yourself (maybe for others, but there is no way to take it with you in the afterlife, so you might as well spend everything). Also, the term $(1 + r)S_t$ is there to indicate that at the end of the year, your savings would have earned you interest at the rate r that you have already used for consumption during the cycle. So,

$$(1+r)S_t + I_{t+1} = C_{t+1}$$

Substituting S_t from (4.1), we get

$$(1+r)(I_t - C_t) + I_{t+1} = C_{t+1}$$

or

$$(1+r)I_t - (1+r)C_t + I_{t+1} = C_{t+1}$$

or

$$(1+r)I_t + I_{t+1} = C_{t+1} + (1-r)C_t$$

or

$$I_t + I_{t+1}/(1+r) = C_{t+1}/(1+r) + C_t$$

This equation is known as the intertemporal budget constraint in economics. While it is used frequently, it rarely is viewed in light of the assumption made. The cycle of value is there to ensure those assumptions ($M = 0$ and $S_{t+1} = 0$) are visible and should be considered when making conclusions or developing economic policies.

4.3 Value as Revenue

In terms of classical economics and in the case of supply and demand, we could see value as revenue, which in its simplest form could be the product of quantity with price (effort, desire, energy loss, etc. excluded). In such a case, we can consider as Value Added the investment per unit times the units produced, as Value Extracted the unit revenue times the units produced, as Value Lost the expenses to produce and sell each unit (labor, equipment, energy, tax, etc.) times the units transacted (equal to the units produced), and as Value Gained the value gained per unit times the units sold (equal to the units produced).

Applying the law of conservation of value, we will get

$$VA + VE = VL + VG$$

For a perfect cycle (quantities will be equal), we can express each value category as a product of money times the number of units circulated. The previous equation will then become

$$\text{Investment} * \text{Units} + \text{Revenue} * \text{Units} = \text{Expenses} * \text{Units} + \text{Gain} * \text{Units}$$

By eliminating the units from both sides of the equation, we get

$$\text{Investment} + \text{Revenue} = \text{Expenses} + \text{Gain}$$

or

$$\text{Gain} - \text{Investment} = \text{Revenue} - \text{Expenses}$$

or

$$\text{Profit} = \text{Revenue} - \text{Expenses}$$

which is a simple accounting expression.

If we are interested in profit maximization, then we can differentiate the previous equation with respect to the quantity of output q and get

$$d(\text{Profit})/dq = (\text{Revenue})' - (\text{Expenses})'$$

or in traditional economic terms

$$d(\text{Profit})/dq = \text{Marginal Revenue} - \text{Marginal Cost}$$

When profit gets maximized, its derivative will be zero. The previous equation then will become a well-known profit maximization equation of economics:

$$\text{Marginal Revenue} = \text{Marginal Cost}$$

At that point, we have that the rate of the extracted value (marginal extracted value) is equal to the rate of the lost value (marginal lost value):

$$VE' = VL'$$

4.4 Value as Information

A final consideration of value for the purposes of this book is to consider information as a proxy to value. Viewing information as a commodity is a challenging endeavor as it creates multiple problems for industrial structure. While its value in economic decision-making is profound, applying it to specific forms of payoff and cost functions can be challenging. Associating information with cost is evident as it takes effort or labor to collect it. While this makes its introduction to economics, natural information poses many challenges as its value is really on the asymmetries it creates.

To be able to use information in an analysis, we need to invent a scale to measure it. Defining a metric for information is not an easy task as information tends to become amorphous in the general case. One could consider the statistical form used in physics and communications where information is seen as a deviation from randomness in a signal, but this definition may be of no economic interest itself since we want to associate it with costs and benefits. For the purposes of this book, we consider information itself can be a product that is bought and sold. The case in point is companies that purchase market research, consumer data, and industry reports to gain a competitive advantage. Creations such as software, books, and patents are forms of information that hold significant economic value. Protecting intellectual property rights ensures that creators can monetize their information products.

In the cycle of value, information will appear as cost. Consider, for example, the case of investing an amount of money X in a company's stock. This becomes our VA. Regardless of the market outcome, at the end of the investment period, we will have extracted VE = rX proportional to the amount we invested. If the proportionality coefficient r is positive, we will end up with VG more than what we have initially invested, while if it is negative, we will have lost money. To make sure we end up with a positive value for r, we invest Y amount of money in acquiring information about the company's future. If the company has developed a new production method that reduces production costs or is about to receive government subsidy, then r will be positive. If, on the other hand, the company is facing a pending lawsuit or negative publicity due to faulty products, then r will be negative.

The law of conservation of value will be

$$VA + VE = VL + VG$$

or

$$X + rX = Y + VG$$

or

$$VG = (1 + r)X - Y$$

When VG > 0, the value of the information we acquired is positive as it contributed to the net gain, while for VG < 0, the information we got was not a reliable predictor of the future.

An interesting, although profound, outcome of the law of conservation of value is when we use it in the form of marginal values. If we take the derivatives of the previous equation with X and Y remaining constant, we get

$$VG' = ((1 + r)X)' - Y'$$

or

$$VG' = Xr'$$

The volatility of the information we got directly influences the volatility of our gained value.

Another case where information enters the value cycle is in the form of reputation. Reputation is nothing more than the accumulation of past information (positive or negative) about an individual, a group, or an organization. Suppose I am a venture capitalist who loans money to a group of entrepreneurs to build their startups. Along with the money I invest, I am also putting my reputation on the line. In case the venture flops, I risk losing my credibility in the industry along with the loss of my investment. My participation might attract other investors based solely on their perception of me as a successful (presumably) investor, which makes my effective value to the startup a lot more than just my monetary contribution. Let us consider that I invest an X amount of money, but due to my reputation, an added amount of rX can also be retrieved from other sources.

In that case, the actual value that I am adding is

$$VA = X + rX$$

After a certain amount of time, the startup is sold, and I receive a share of Y money, while the investors who followed me gain rY. That amount would also be value gained for me but in the form of reputation. I can monetize this amount if at some point I ask an investor to join me in another venture.

4.5 Value as Need: An Exploration

One thing we seem to forget in economic theory is that not all entities are "cylinders" (as depicted in figures up to now). Everything

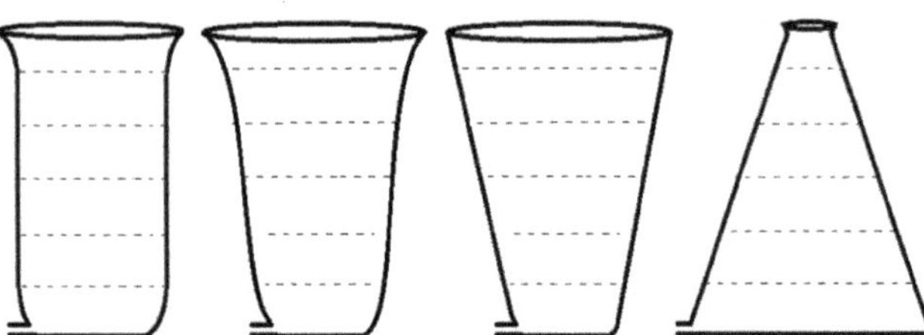

Figure 4.3. Abstract representation of economic entities.

comes in different shapes or vessels (Figure 4.3) at the individual, organizational, government, and society levels. Also, we are not completely sealed or closed as systems. For our functioning, we require different amounts of value based on our present and future needs. What traditional economics and its modern variants such as biophysical economics often miss is that there is a hierarchy of needs that shapes our appreciation and need for value. For example, at the individual level, we first need physiological value, such as the water we drink and the food we eat. The air we breathe is also of value, especially when it is "clean" of pollutants. For organizations, this first level of value can come in the form of earnings that ensure survival or sustainable growth, while at the society level, we need value in the form of security from external or internal threat, such as having an army to protect us against external threats and policy to ensure internal safety.

An important aspect here is how the entities we discussed weigh their various needs in terms of the value they need to invest or add to satisfy them. Naturally, safety is more important than pleasure (rationally thinking) and so we would expect that activities to ensure safety take priority over any higher-order needs, such as entertainment and self-actualization. This suggests the notion of the hierarchy of needs that usually appears in theories of developmental psychology. A classic representative of this case is the hierarchy of needs that Maslow developed in 1943. In his scheme, which we also adopt and extend here for individuals and organizations, a description of human motivation is outlined in terms of fulfillment of needs in order of their importance for one's survival and growth. Starting from the basic and fundamental needs to the emotional and then to the more conceptual and abstract, the various levels of needs for individuals include the following:

- **Physiological:** necessary for the functioning of the human body, such as food, water, air for metabolism, clothing and shelter for protection from the elements, and sex for reproduction and sustainment of the species.
- **Safety:** from infrequent natural and human events such as natural disasters, social disruptions such as economic crises and various forms of violence and abuse.
- **Social:** involving interpersonal needs, such as feelings of belonging, acceptance, intimacy, friendship, and love.
- **Cognitive:** including the desire to be accepted and valued by others in social, professional, and personal settings. In simple terms, it's the need to make a positive impact on other people's lives. The value of this need can be measured by the self-esteem and self-respect one has for themselves.
- **Self-actualization:** the need to realize one's full potential and accomplish everything that one can.

To Maslow's list, we add one more that expresses the need for someone to be something beyond what they are:

- **Legacy:** the need to be remembered as something important and significant to the lives of future generations. Perpetuating in the memory of others in time is an important drive that is not directly addressed by the other needs.

Although, as a trigger and motivator of actions, legacy could be considered as part of self-actualization and cognitive needs, we believe it deserves a separate mention as the motivations behind it are different since it addresses "metaphysical" needs. Being accepted by others as a cognitive need could potentially include legacy, but the level of reward and feedback one gets from the fulfillment of a cognitive need is directly perceived by the individual, while the notion of legacy, at least from the individual's point of view, is purely a mental dimension that can differ in expression from a cognitive need. In addition, reaching one's full potential is personal and private and has a mark or a point in time beyond which there is nothing more anyone needs or should want to do.

Leaving a legacy is a need that projects the impression that the individual in some sense will perpetuate in time in the minds of others. For example, while a cognitive need might trigger one to donate to charity, a legacy need might drive them to create a fund that will provide ongoing help and support to a cause past and beyond their lifetime. Seeking breakthroughs is another example of legacy need as it addresses the need to go beyond the recognition of the living and extend to the future past the individual's life. Wanting to be remembered, say like Einstein, Beethoven, or Michelangelo, is something that the need for legacy tries to distinctly encapsulate.

The importance of legacy in economics is not easily seen as we typically do not consider individuals when studying the economy. For some reason, we seem to forget that organizations, governments, and even the market are run by influential and powerful individuals whose decision-making style is strongly influenced by their personality, achievements, and needs. The political and business scenes are abundant with leaders who took down their organizations and even their economies or countries.

Given the identified list of needs, the view of the value cycle should change into a dynamic one where value comes and goes in a continuous cycle. Figure 4.4 displays this dynamic nature with values coming from different sources in the container representing an agent. To gain value, the agent "invests" by contributing VA to retrieve

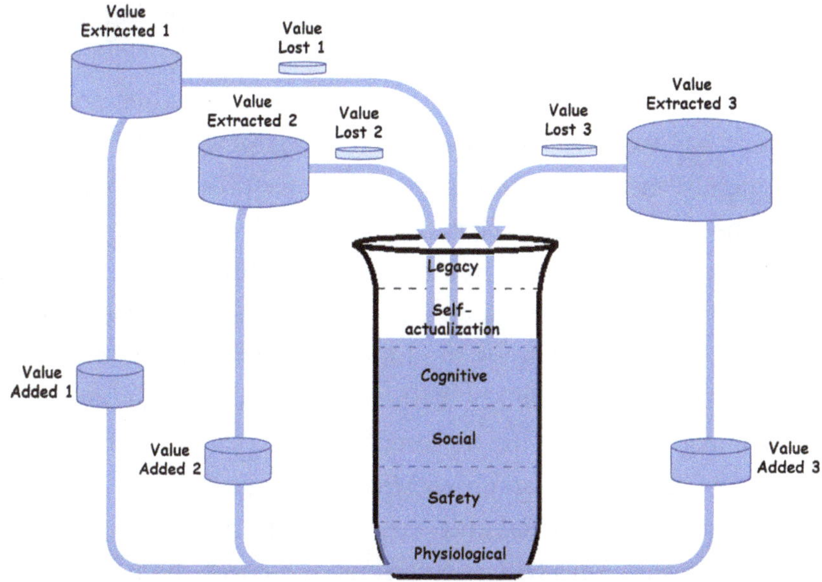

Figure 4.4.   The dynamic nature of needs and values.

the VE. Each value cycle can operate at different timescales so what we see in the agent container of Figure 4.4 is the cumulative result of all the cycling processes at an instant in time. The whole system balances the process at each point in time at a certain level in the container with the goal of the agent being to fill its container "self".

Agents need to constantly keep fulfilling their needs if they are to stay "alive" and rise in the hierarchy of needs. As long as the inflow matches the outflow, we can remain in a steady state of equilibrium. If, say, the economy is not doing well (suppressive environment) and individuals lose their jobs, the inflow will be less than the outflow and their physiological and safety needs will be at risk. When eventually their activities (VA contributions) become "profitable", the surplus of inflow will raise the level of the "liquid" in their container and higher-order needs will be satisfied. If the agents don't manage to sustain their level of needs and are continuously losing value, the rewards (traces of food probably) might barely be enough to cover their physiological needs, risking the potential emptying of their vessel and death.

Of course, everyone is different from one another and has different life experiences and perceptions of themselves, and consequently, the breadth or depth of each person's needs will vary. In our discussion here, we consider the needs as the parts of the internal capital that drive the flow of value through the network of the traits and attributes of an individual while being themselves attributes. Figure 4.5 shows the hierarchy of needs for different individuals as represented by different shapes of containers. The left container is closer to the representation of a hierarchy that most people are familiar with and how Maslow imagined it.

Differences in the social and natural environment one is raised in and functions along with the various influences she experiences allow different amounts of needs to be satisfied. The more able an individual, or in our case an economy, is and the more opportunities the environment provides, the more needs they can fulfill (liquid level in Figure 4.5) and the higher up they are in the hierarchy. Satisfying needs is like filling a bucket of water that has a hole at the bottom. There is a constant demand for value from the environment each agent operates.

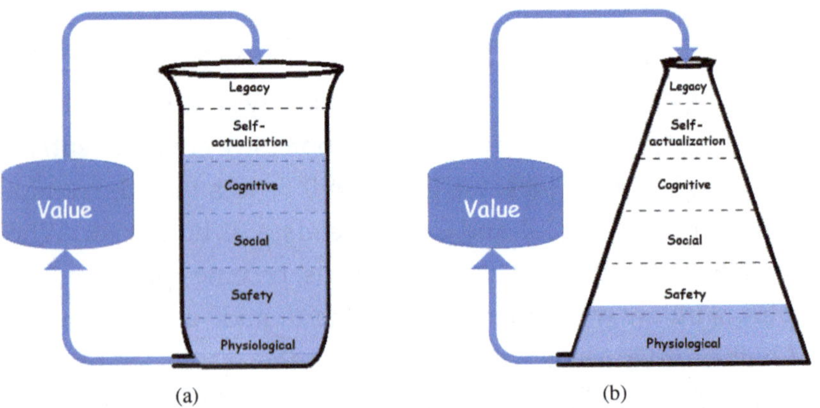

Figure 4.5. Needs and values for different containers.

Some individuals have low physiological needs compared to others and the opposite might be so at higher levels. In these cases, the accumulation of value will raise its level in the container at different speeds leading to faster or slower satisfaction of the various needs. Figure 4.6 provides a visual representation of the gained value in terms of its level in the containers. Each of the three cases of gained value will have its own cycle of value and in all three of them the gained value is the same and increasing at the same rate. Due to the different shape of their containers, one (individual) might be at safety level (rightmost), another at the social level (middle), and yet another (leftmost) at the cognitive level.

Something that is beyond the scope of this book and more in the realm of philosophy is that this hierarchy of needs is not set in

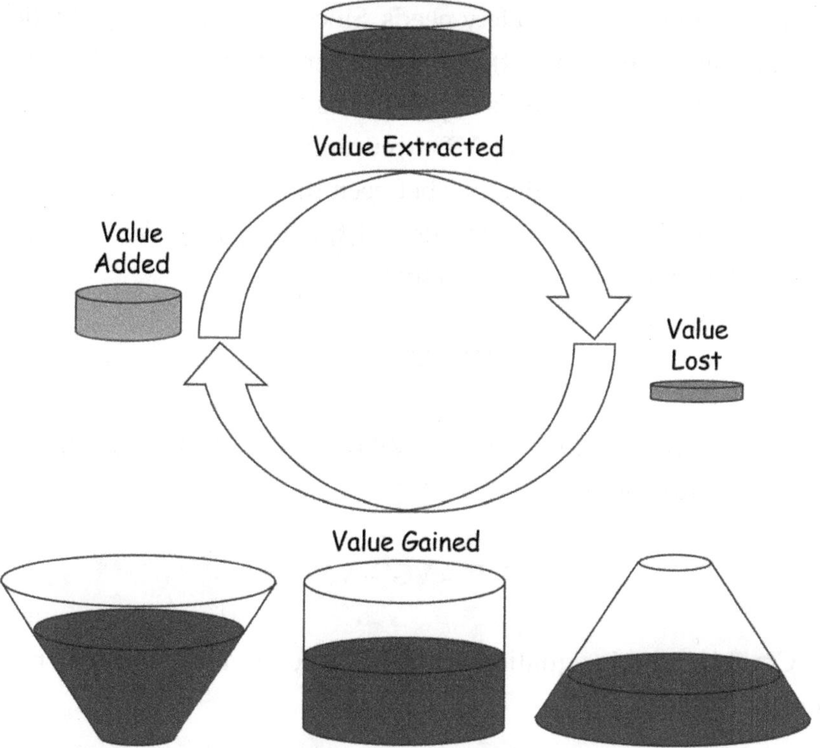

Figure 4.6. Value containers.

stone, and for some reason, human beings and the organizations and institutions they lead have the amazing capacity to shift them up and down according to their state and the situations they are facing. Consider, for example, the extreme case of a Buddhist monk who meditates in isolation. His social needs are apparently zero, while his self-actualization needs have transcended to another level. Similarly, while his physiological needs remain, the need for safety is not of primal importance to him. This person could very well be an exceptional leader if he wanted to, but he is content and happy with his own choice.

To demonstrate how the hierarchy of needs can be used, let's assume here the case of an agent whose needs are represented with the container of Figure 4.7. Apparently, the specific agent is not wealthy as he can barely satisfy his physiological needs while struggling to satisfy his safety needs. Since it is a dynamic situation (value flowing in and out), we study here the rate of satisfaction of the need or value that is expressed as the rate of change of the total value (Value Total, or VT) accumulated over time. This will be dependent on the difference between the rate of incoming value (Value In, or VI) in the container and the outgoing (Value Out, or VO) that is invested as added value:

$$VT' = VI' - VO'$$

In terms of the cycle of value, $VI' = VG'$ and $VO' = VA'$. So, the previous equation will become

$$VT' = VG' - VA'$$

Combining this equation with the cycle of value in the form of marginal values

$$VA' + VE' = VL' + VG'$$

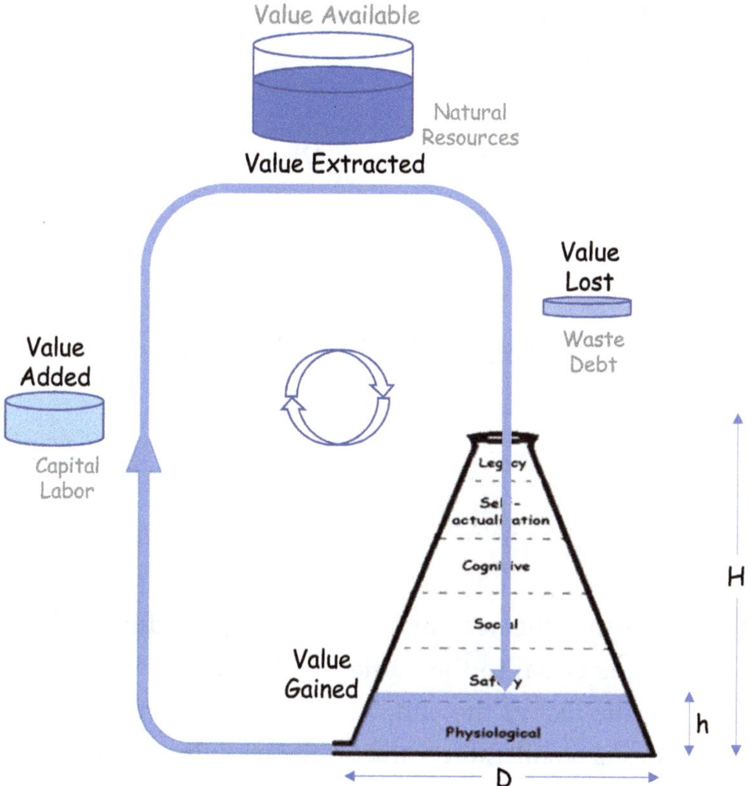

Figure 4.7. Value as needed.

we get

$$VT' = VE' - VL'$$

If we now consider the neoclassical assumption that the Value Extracted is abundant (maybe the agent has a steady income from a job), then

$$VE' = 0$$

so

$$VT' = -VL'$$

By integrating this equation between a beginning time t_1 and an ending time t_2, we get

$$\int_{t_1}^{t_2} VT = -\int_{t_1}^{t_2} VL$$

or

$$VTt_2 - VTt_1 = VLt_1 - VLt_2$$

or

$$\Delta(VT) = VLt_1 - VLt_2$$

This means that the accumulated value $\Delta(VT)$ during the time interval $t_2 - t_1$ is equal to the value that we lost at the beginning minus the value lost at the end. As long as the amount of value that we lose gets smaller, the value in the container will be getting higher. The result does not say anything directly about the value VA we invest. One would expect that the more we invest (VA′ > 0), the more we would extract. This is only possible if there is more value to extract. In the case of being employed this could happen when by adding more work (either quantity or quality), we end up being promoted to a position with higher salary.

Readers who want to expand more can try different geometric shapes for the agent container and see how the height of value h can be expressed in terms of time and Value Lost. For example, if we assume that the structure of the agent container is a cone (Figure 4.7) with base diameter D and height H, then the volume of the whole container is

$$V = \frac{1}{3}\pi \left(\frac{D}{2}\right)^2 H$$

To avoid complicated mathematical expressions, we consider the general expression for the volume of the shaded area in the container (Figure 4.7) as a function of h, H, and D, with h, as a function of time $h(t)$. So,

$$V = f(h(t), H, D)$$

In a more abstract form, it would be

$$VT = f(h(t, \text{Shape}))$$

where Shape is some expression of the shape of the container.

What we are interested in here is how fast VT (the volume of value) changes with time, especially if the rate of change is positive or negative. In other words, we are interested in the marginal value of VT which is nothing but the first derivative of VT:

$$VT' = [f(h(t, \text{Shape}))]'$$

or

$$VT' = f'(h(t, \text{Shape}))*h'(t)$$

Combining this with the cycle of value in its marginal form for an abundant source of value, we eventually (follow the steps we did before and) get

$$f'(h(t, \text{Shape}))*h'(t) = -VL'$$

It can be evident here how challenging it would be to integrate this complex form to get a more easily expressed result. This showcases the complexities of simulating economic entities and transactions in real life. To account for the individual deviations when we consider large populations, we typically assume they can be represented mathematically by a probability distribution of the variable we want to study (value in our case). For example, the need for safety might be low and high for a few individuals, while the majority would be expected to fall around a mean. One way to simulate large populations is by adopting the normal distribution (in its standardized form) as representing the safety variable. The mean of zero could represent indifference toward safety, with positive values indicating a greater need for safety, while negative values could represent less need for safety. Figure 4.8 shows some possibilities that might exist for various populations. The area under the sections of the curve indicates the percentage of the population whose variable is within the limits of the section.

The appeal of the normal distribution stems from, among others, the fact that most distributions that represent social entities will approach the normal curve for large populations and its simplicity in requiring only two parameters (μ and σ) for its description. The former fact is key in developing the central limit theorem,

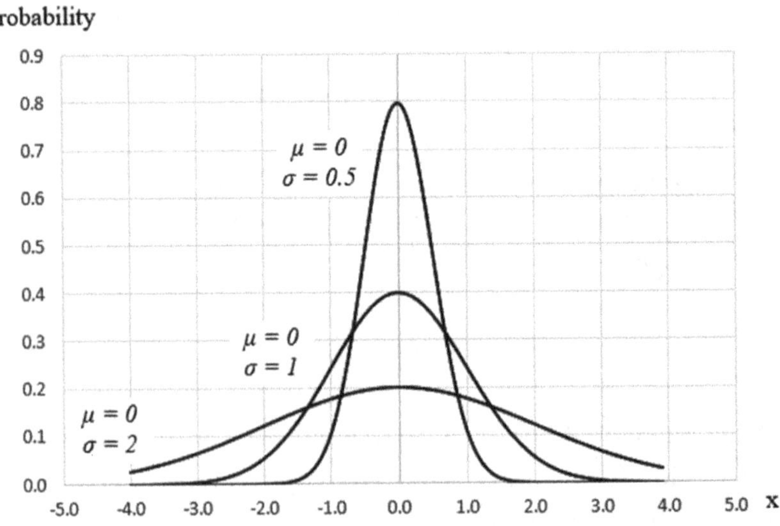

Figure 4.8. Normal distribution.

while the latter makes it "easy" to work with in statistics (most statistical techniques depend on distributions being normal). An additional advantage is that it allows comparison between dissimilar entities (metaphorically such as apples and oranges) by using the standardized form where the horizontal axis becomes the z value axis. By converting everything to their z value, we can compare the various categories of needs.

While the value one assigns to something will generally be different from the value someone else assigns, on average, and as a society or economy, most will agree on the number we will place on value for a certain event, such as the acquisition of a product. We need to make clear here something that we said in previous sections, that value is not price. Although price, or to be more precise the price one is willing to pay, can represent to an extent value, it falls short in accounting for the effort and satisfaction one puts on top of paying the price. The value one places on something is standard although different for each one of us. In terms of individuals, it is more like height. Some are tall, some are short, and most are in the middle. The individual height of each one of us does not change (let's agree within days), but as a group, it will most probably follow some form of distribution that closely resembles the normal distribution.

When individuals engage in exchanges to acquire something (material or spiritual), they play the role of a consumer. In such cases, they are driven by their needs. To satisfy their needs, they must gain value, so they engage in value cycles. The analogy with the container of needs we use in this book is depicted in Figure 4.9 where we have three different individuals or containers (same shape for simplicity) at various stages of satisfying their needs (the height of each segment or need is kept the same for simplicity). The leftmost container represents a poor individual who can barely manage their physiological needs (food, water, health, etc.), while the rightmost container represents a rich individual who has satisfied their (perceived) needs and just considers what they are going to leave

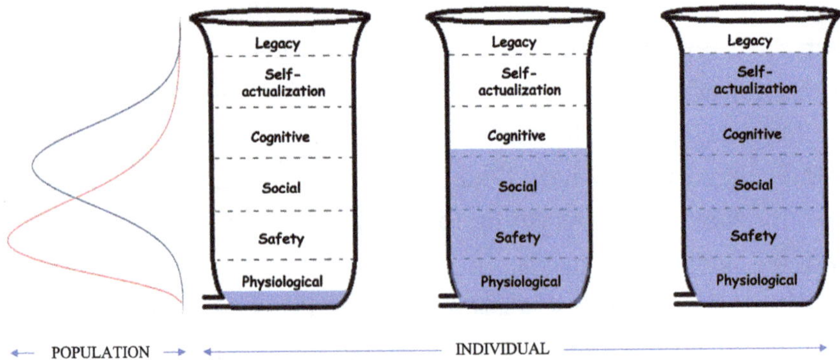

Figure 4.9.   Value levels.

behind. Finally, in the middle, we have an "average" individual who has satisfied their basic needs and looks to satisfy their more spiritual needs.

While for individuals their needs might be satisfied at different levels in the hierarchy of needs, we would expect that at the society or economy level, they would aggregate around a mean, let's say measured in *valuemeters* (creative license applied here). For an underdeveloped economy, we would expect that mean to be closer to the bottom of the hierarchy (red curve in Figure 4.10), while for a developing economy, it would be near the middle (blue curve in Figure 4.10).

By analogy to physics where we cannot predict the microstates of single atoms in a gas, but we can predict the collective behavior in terms of parameters like temperature, pressure, and volume, here we cannot predict the behavior of individuals, but collectively we might be able to predict their behavior at the economy level, assumed as a closed system. Knowing the value distribution for a product in an economy can allow us to plan a market strategy or perform a feasibility study for the sales we could anticipate. Figure 4.10 depicts the distributions of a hypothetical product in two economies A and B in terms of the need it targets. Economy A seems to be more affluent at least with respect to its hierarchy of needs. Considering the value

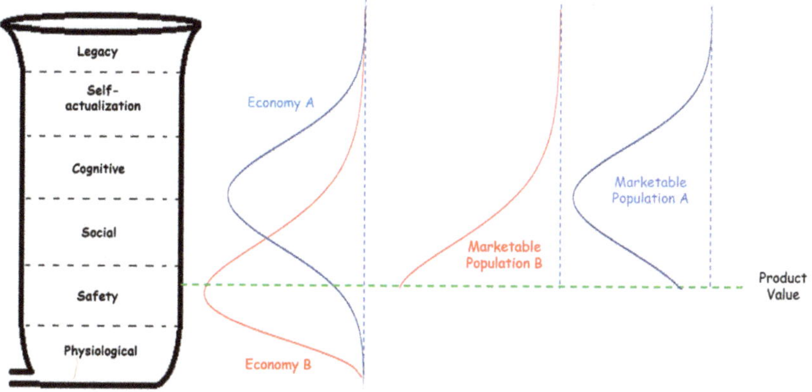

Figure 4.10. Value distributions and the hierarchy of needs.

of our product at the safety level (dashed green horizontal line) of the hierarchy of needs, we can see that the proportion of the population (area under the curve) that can afford this value is higher in A than in B (labeled marketable population). The inquiring reader can expand on how frequency distributions can be used in the context of the law of conservation of value.

Scaling up from the individual to the organization, the needs can be similar. For example, organizations need cash flow (physiological needs) to meet their obligations (paying wages, commissions, taxes, etc.). They also like to be safe (safety needs) from the threat of competitors, appeal to their industries and the societies they operate in (social needs), innovate to satisfy their creative nature (cognitive needs), and express their capabilities to the fullest (self-actualization needs). They also reach a stage where they want to give back to ensure their historic presence (legacy needs). Similarly, one can devise a hierarchy of needs for governments and the societies they represent.

5

VALUE AND ENERGY

A very popular proxy for value that we didn't consider in the previous chapter is energy. Energy plays a fundamental role in economic thought by serving as input in the production of goods and services. Its association with value has been explored from various theoretical perspectives, each emphasizing different aspects of the energy–value relationship. From an enabler of labor, to a factor of cost, to a fundamental driver of economic activity, understanding the association between value and energy is crucial in formulating policies that aim for sustainable development and efficient resource allocation.

From a physical perspective, one can see the analogy of the cycle of value to a form of energy conservation. As Figure 5.1 depicts, we can assume that the VE and the VG are static or state characteristics in the sense that they represent something that exists at a certain instance in time, suggesting, by analogy to physics, that they play the role of potential energy (EP). On the other hand, VA and VL represent value flow through time and as such can be analogous to kinetic energy (EK). When an object in physics moves from one position to another in a conservative force field, we can say that according to the law of conservation of energy,

$$EK_1 + EP_1 = EK_2 + EP_2$$

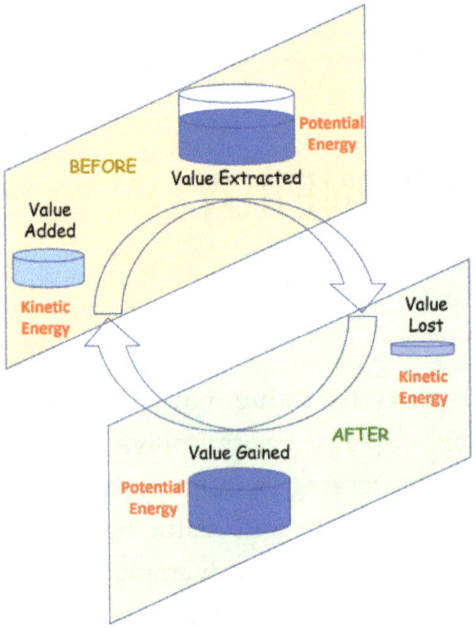

Figure 5.1. The conservation of energy as value.

By analogy (Figure 5.1), we get

$$VA + VE = VG + VL$$

which is what we have already established as the law of conservation of value in equation (1.1).

A necessary clarification is required here in that the VG and VE are not exactly state quantities but rather differences of state quantities. For the whole process to start, we must have had some initial amount of value (Value Initial) available to us as potential or labor or capital. From that we diverted some as VA to the transformation process and eventually ended up with a final amount (Value Final) of value. So,

$$\text{Value Gained} = \text{Value Final} - \text{Value Initial}$$

Similarly, the VE is the difference from what was initially available (for example, in nature) minus what we leave after the extraction process. These "differences" are analogous to the potential energy in physics as we always measure potential with respect to a reference point. For example, when it comes to gravitational potential, we sometimes use the surface of the Earth as our zero point or level, while other times we consider its center.

If one takes the analogy between value and energy a little further, then we can consider the Lagrangian of the value (L) (seen as action potential here) as the difference between the transferred Value Added/Lost (similar to kinetic energy) and Value Extracted/Gained (similar to potential energy).

In classical mechanics,

$$L = EK_1 + EK_2 - EP_1 - EP_2$$

which in our case will become

$$L = VA + VL - VE - VG$$

Let's consider a simple example to demonstrate the application of L in the case of value. Assuming a simplified linear form for value as a function of product quantity (q) in a cycle of value, then we can have

$$V = k*q$$

where k is a proportionality constant (could be also seen as price). So,

$$VA = k_A*q$$
$$VL = k_L*q$$
$$VE = k_E*q$$
$$VG = k_G*q$$

If one wants to see the analogy to real life, k_A could be the manufacturing cost per unit produced, k_L could be the cost of transportation or distribution (including expenses such as insurances and taxes) per unit produced, k_E could be the profit made per unit produced, and k_G could be the gain per unit produced. The Lagrangian in this case will become

$$L = k_A{}^*q + k_L{}^*q - k_E{}^*q - k_G{}^*q$$

or

$$L = (k_A + k_L - k_E - k_G) \times q$$

Then, we can even apply the principle of least action that states that a system will follow a path from its initial state (VE here) to its final (VG here) so that the difference the Lagrangian expresses is minimal. This situation is expressed through the second-order Lagrange equation (also called Euler–Lagrange equation):

$$\frac{\theta L}{\theta q} - \frac{d}{dt}\left(\frac{\theta L}{\theta q'}\right) = 0$$

Calculating the partial derivatives in our case will produce

$$\frac{\theta L}{\theta q} = k_A + k_L - k_E - k_G$$

Since our Lagrangian does not include the derivative of the quantity over time,

$$\frac{d}{dt}\left(\frac{\theta L}{\theta q'}\right) = 0$$

So,

$$k_A + k_L - k_E - k_G = 0$$

or

$$k_A + k_L = k_E + k_G$$

which states that the most efficient cycles happen when the VA per production unit (VA_p) plus the VL per production unit (VL_p) is equal to the VE per production unit (VE_p) plus the VG per production unit (VG_p). Considering one production unit ($q = 1$), the last equation becomes

$$VA_p + VL_p = VE_p + VG_p$$

If we consider the cycle of value for one production unit, the law of conservation of value becomes

$$VA_p + VE_p = VG_p + VL_p$$

By adding the last two equations, we get

$$2 \times VA_p = 2 \times VG_p$$

or

$$VA_p = VG_p$$

For linear value functions, the most efficient cycles are achieved when the value we add per production unit is equal to the value we gain per production unit. In other words, you can't gain more than what you add (you can't get something out of nothing), at least when only quantities are considered. While this result does not showcase something radical as it is profound in nature, it does serve as foundational support for the validity of the law of conservation of value in representing economic situations.

5.1 Thermodynamic Analogy

An alternative view of the cycle of value is to see it in the form of the first law of thermodynamics where the work (W) done by an isolated system plus the heat added to the system (Q) is equal to the change of its internal energy (ΔU). Figure 5.2(a) depicts the first law of thermodynamics for a gas in a container that produces work when heated. Expressed as an equation, the law becomes

$$\Delta U = W + Q \tag{5.1}$$

In the case of the cycle of value (Figure 5.2(b)), the system that experiences the state change is nature. To preserve the analogy with

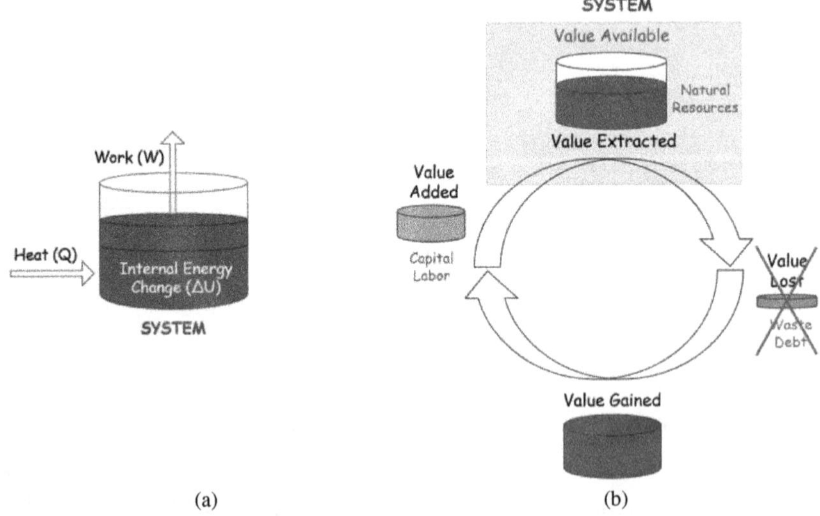

Figure 5.2. Thermodynamic view of the cycle of value.

the first law of thermodynamics, we will assume that nature is a closed system, so we have no losses (VL = 0). In that case, what we contribute as Q is the VA and what the system gives us as W is the VG. What has changed in nature is that its value has been decreased by the VE amount that represents the difference between the value that was available in nature and the value that is left after our extraction. Equation (5.1) in our case will become

$$VE = VG + VA$$

which is the law of conservation of value as expressed by equation (1.1) without VL.

The second law of thermodynamics states that the entropy (S) of a closed system always increases. As entropy here, we will consider the state of disorder in a system. The term disorder is used as an encapsulation of the size of the configuration space (number of combinations available). Larger configuration spaces (ways to arrange something) equal larger entropy. The equivalent information-centric approach of the entropy will be left for a future analysis. The law can be expressed as

$$\Delta S \geq 0 \tag{5.2}$$

There are multiple ways we can see entropy in terms of the cycle of value, with the simplest one being as an additive quantity that describes the ease with which value can be added. For example, the total value of an individual at a point in time could be their sum of bank deposits, credit score, reputation, stocks, skill set, physical strength, property they own, etc. Each one of these sources of value is a form of value that they can "liquidate" as added value to access an external value pool. The difference is that some of these forms are "easier" to engage in the value cycle than others. For instance, if a product needs to be purchased, then with little physical effort one can transfer money from their bank account to the seller and acquire that product. We can say that in this case the entropy of the value used was high (ordered, in entropy lingo) and it took very little to produce useful work. In general, one would expect that using cash to acquire value is faster than using credit (applying for a loan) or exerting physical effort like getting a job to make the money to pay for the product.

For the same amount of VG, different types of VA will contribute different entropy quantities. Considering a hypothetical exchange scenario between a buyer and a seller and focusing only on effort, cash, and product, we will have for the buyer (the superscript b is for the buyer)

$$\Delta S^b_{total} = \Delta S^b_{effort} + \Delta S^b_{cash} + \Delta S^b_{product}$$

and for the seller (the superscript s is for the seller)

$$\Delta S^s_{total} = \Delta S^s_{effort} + \Delta S^s_{cash} + \Delta S^s_{product}$$

By adding these two equations, we get

$$\Delta S^b_{total} + \Delta S^s_{total} = \Delta S^b_{effort} + \Delta S^b_{cash} + \Delta S^b_{product} + \Delta S^s_{effort} + \Delta S^s_{cash} + \Delta S^s_{product}$$

ΔS^b_{cash} and ΔS^s_{cash} are equal but opposite (one loses while the other gains the money), so they cancel out in the previous equation. The same goes for the product components, so the previous equation now becomes

$$\Delta S^b_{total} + \Delta S^s_{total} = \Delta S^b_{effort} + \Delta S^s_{effort}$$

The total entropy change of the process becomes

$$\Delta S = \Delta S^b_{effort} + \Delta S^s_{effort}$$

Given that both buyer and seller make or exert effort, their disorder increased. So, ΔS^b_{effort} and ΔS^s_{effort} are positive. So,

$$\Delta S^b_{effort} + \Delta S^s_{effort} \geq 0$$

or

$$\Delta S \geq 0$$

The entropy for the buyer and seller system increased. There is a lot more that can go into this discussion, especially when one considers entropy from an information point of view (information can act as a proxy to value as we saw in the previous chapter), but for the time being, displaying the application of the second law of thermodynamics with the simple buyer–seller system demonstrates its applicability to the cycle of value.

EPILOGUE

An attempt was made in this book to provide a framework for studying the economy based on the assumption that value as potential to act in an environment is conserved in closed economic systems. This assumption led to the formulation of the law of conservation of value where value added or invested, and value extracted equal the value lost and value gained. As a result of this formulation, typical economic qualities like marginal utility and the law of diminishing marginal utility are replaced with marginal value and speed of marginal value in the analysis.

Takeaways of the law of conservation of value in economics include the following:

- The sum total of all economic value within a closed economic system does not change over time. Nature can be part of the cycle when appropriate and appears as value gained when we extract value from natural resources or as value lost when we return waste to it.
- Economic value can be transformed from one form to another (e.g., from raw materials to finished goods) but the total value remains the same.
- Value cannot be created out of nothing, nor can it vanish; it can only change hands or forms. Innovation in this respect is nothing more than the flow of value from one form, typically

intellectual potential and the will of individuals, their collaborative capabilities, and resources into another (new product or service).

This concept challenges traditional economic theories where value is often created through production, innovation, and services, leading to economic growth.

The "value" of expressing economic activity as a law of conservation of value comes from the simplification of economic modeling and the enforcement of a way of thinking that always considers losses of some form (capital, utility, etc.). Tracking economic activity becomes more straightforward when total value is conserved, simplifying national accounting and financial reporting. Policymakers could also more accurately predict the outcomes of economic policies when the total value remains constant.

Another advantage of applying the law of conservation of value is in enhancing economic stability. With a fixed total value, economic fluctuations like booms and busts could be anticipated and action to minimize their impact can be planned, leading to a more stable economy. Speculations about the creation of new value can also be reduced and the impact of speculative bubbles driven by perceived (but unrealistic) increases in value restrained.

One can even see the law as a mitigator of inequalities and as limiting wealth concentration. If the value cannot be infinitely accumulated, it may lead to a more equitable distribution of wealth. Excessive accumulation of value by a small segment of the population could also be prevented, potentially reducing economic disparities. By focusing on value reallocation as a society, we can achieve efficiency improvements that emphasize sustainability. Maybe businesses and governments could split some of their focus on reallocating existing value more efficiently rather than creating new value.

The application of the law of conservation of value to the producer–consumer scenario, as well as the market and economy levels, reveals some already known realities as outcomes of formulations and not through intuition. As a result, the use of the formulas developed here can form the basis for further analysis. The recommendation for future research on economic theory would be to ensure that variables chosen to represent value should comply with the law of conservation of value as presented here. This ensures the accounting of the various value terms is properly balanced out. Above all, the intention of the development of the law of conservation of value was to provide a framework for thinking holistically about economic systems and one that makes the assumptions we make prominent.

APPENDIX: A BRIEF HISTORY OF VALUE IN ECONOMIC THOUGHT

Human interaction has been studied throughout the centuries where models of value, motivation, and rational choice have been customized to address the intricacies of the market as perceived at the time. Value is typically seen as the currency of needs or wants as one is trying to satisfy them. The market in this respect acts like Eden where all needs can be satisfied. Rational choices are assumed in interactions even when some might appear "irrational" at first. This is due to the complexity of the human psyche; a masochist finds high value in being punished, whereas a "normal" person finds low value (presumably negative) and would try to avoid it. Others could find value in the joy of abusing others, so a sadist-masochist dyad makes a dysfunctional couple psychologically an ideal pair in economics.

What enables rationality, at least from an economic perspective, is a common measure of value for every option that influences an exchange. Without a near-common understanding of value, it would be impossible to anticipate and plan a negotiation and action strategy to engage in an exchange. A producer and a consumer need to have the same or at least a similar understanding of value if they are to interact. A factory functions by assuming the same product that it mass produces will cover the needs of many. There is a clear understanding that the value the product adds to consumers is the same for all of them enabling in this way the streamlining of a production process to gain efficiencies of scale.

The way value perceptions form and are shared in a group of people is core among establishments like the government and religion. At the scale of the economy and market, a critical assumption is made that the individual is truly "individual" or otherwise independent from influences. There is a contradiction here as oftentimes the influence of others is what creates or adds value to something – fashion is a case in point. So, the assumption that one is freely forming and expressing his rational preferences is an idealization aiming at satisfying the law of averages that is a true reflection of real instances of interactions. In the market context, the assumption becomes that someone is not influenced by what others buy. While this is a convenient simplification to develop workable equations and formulas, it is far from reality. Ignoring social norms and the dialogs we have with each other is like treating everyone in isolation and looks more like a dystopian post-apocalyptic world than the reality we live and function in now.

Regardless of the limitations imposed by the simplifications and abstractions we make, an approximation is far better than ignorance which can paralyze decision-making and planning. Assuming a qualitative similarity in value allows for a quantitative expression of our exchanges and the buildup of mathematical expressions to represent them. Such expressions suffer from a monistic view of value and isolate individual acts in exchange for single properties of value.

To avoid the limitations of the "traditional" view, alternatives have been proposed where multiple forms of value are considered. Being rational now becomes a matter of intelligibly expressing our needs to others through shared norms established by dialog and consensus of everyone forming a market or exchange. Such socially grounded views can allow for the incorporation of ethics as a value and value-shaping construct.

One of the first writings where a form of value appears is in Aristotle's *Nicomachean Ethics*. That is where Aristotle discusses gain and loss in a voluntary exchange as having more or less than what one owns. Owning something has a certain "use value" or usefulness in fulfilling its intended purpose to satisfy a need. In this way, a house is valued due to the way we use it to satisfy needs, such as protection from the elements and privacy. A pair of shoes is of value too as they protect our feet from the elements and allow us to move more efficiently. The values of the house and the shoes are different because they are used differently. For a fair exchange to take place, some sort of proportionality needs to be achieved because one pair of shoes, in the greatest majority of circumstances, cannot possibly be equated to a house. Since one quantity is exchanged for a different one, Aristotle introduces the concept of reciprocity as mutual benefit. This he considers as the glue that holds people together.

To explain his stance, Aristotle presents the example of a builder who makes a house and a shoemaker who makes a shoe. For a fair exchange between the two, there must be equivalency in terms of the benefits they gain. Since it is difficult to establish how many pairs of shoes are equivalent to a house, a way must be devised to make the things that are exchanged comparable. The concept of "exchange value" in the form of money is introduced to act as an intermediary or common denominator in the transaction. As such, money becomes by convention a sort of representative of demand. This is the reason the actual word for money in Greek is *nomisma* (νόμισμα) which is derived from the word *nomos* meaning by law. It is not something that exists in nature but by law and it is in our power to change it and make it useless if we want.

So, what appears as gain and loss is nothing more than the conversion of one form of value into another. "That demand holds things together as a single unit is shown by the fact that when men do not need one another, i.e., when neither needs the other or one does not need the other, they do not exchange". Money is there to make sure that if something is needed in the future, it can be acquired. Now, considering money as another form of good exposes it to the volatility of any other good which is affected by supply and demand. The difference, according to Aristotle, is that money is steadier or at least as steady as the government that produced it. Considering that governments are "representatives" of the people, they inherit the trust of the societies they serve and by extension, the money they produce are expressions of the same trust that holds societies together. In this way, justice is effective in exchanges and ethics is introduced.

In Aristotle's thought, money becomes the equalizer of value and in essence, it is what makes objects and services commensurable. In the form of reciprocity, Aristotle attributes objects and services to a capacity of exchanging. This "property" allows the quantification of exchanges as proportions. Alternatively, one can see that objects and services have intrinsic capacities or value in the form of causal power. The solution to the problem of commensurability is solved at the level of government by the introduction of money and at the level of the individual as need or want.

Following Aristotle's treatise on economics, we have a complete absence of significant contributions during the rise of the Roman empire and later the Christian association of exchanges with levels of sins during the Middle Ages. This gave rise to the guild system where value was equated to just price, seen here as proportional to one's status in society. When a price is not fixed by authorities, then a producer should do as much as is necessary to maintain his social status but no more. When considering a competitive market, then this means to refer to a common estimation of the price in such a market. Saint Thomas Aquinas makes a distinction with respect to arbitrage stating that while it is not a mortal sin to capitalize on an opportunity, it would be more virtuous to share knowledge that would eliminate the arbitrage before engaging in an exchange.

As reformation followed the Middle Ages, and the influence of the Catholic church declined, national identities began to form. Nations began to accumulate wealth and precious metals such as gold and silver became proxies for value. This led to the economic theory and practice of mercantilism where government policies aimed at encouraging exports and discouraging imports, so wealth stays within the boundaries of the nation. Later, more valuable goods began to gain importance. A case in point was the trade mediated between England and India through the East India Company. As Thomas Mun, a director of the company, stated while England would export or pay India in gold and silver, it would acquire spices and cloths of various kinds from India that would subsequently sell for great profit in Europe and other areas enhancing this way a positive flow of money for England. Specialized goods also became the currency of value expanding the narrow of mercantilism that only gold and silver were the only forms of wealth.

As new forms of value are introduced, one should never forget that nations in those days were always under the threat of war, and for such situations, they had to always rely on value that could be converted to war supplies as fast as possible. In that respect, precious metals never lost their appeal as repositories of wealth. Coins, on the other hand, often experienced debasement as rulers would clip them, pollute their silver content or claim value on the stamp they would place on them. John Locke objected to this practice as it contributed to the diminution of the things a coin could buy resulting in this way in increasing prices.

Locke also contributed to economic thought as he saw value as labor, in that the labor one puts into an activity justifies them to take ownership of the outcomes. For example, if one makes the effort to collect acorns in moderation to his needs, then he is entitled ownership to of those acorns. Excesses should be avoided as socially undesirable. Similarly, if one makes the effort to clear a plot of land that does not belong to anyone, then he is entitled to keep it. God presumably gave earth to all mankind so labor would be claimed to it by individuals. Although this might sound extreme in our days, we must not forget that at the times of Locke white people were spreading throughout North America that was considered free land for taking. This helped develop a labor theory of property. Given that by convention and through a social contract people agreed to use money as a measure of value, money can be used to buy land. We see here how the value can be expressed in terms of labor, land, and money in the form of precious metals. In this way, using money addressed the ethical and religious concerns of that time (17th century) were addressed.

During the same period, Hume developed his ideas on the moral justification of property as a "natural" instinct that changes by evolution and the notion of public utility. Hume also sees money as a "representation of labor and commodities and serves only as a method of rating or estimating them". Above all, though, Hume views labor as value and even points out how the division of labor leads to an increase in value. The breakdown of production was emphasized by Adam Smith in the 18th century where the value added by different specialized individuals in the assembly line of a product is much higher than if the same number of generalist individuals were each separately producing one product each.

The division of labor capitalizes on the increased dexterity of every particular workman (it is easier to specialize and become an expert in a small task than a complicated one). Imagine a series of specialized people in an assembly line building a car and a single enthusiast building one in their garage. Despite the intention and skill that an individual might have, it cannot compete with the specialization of skill of the assembly line of specialized people. Additionally, the passing from one stage to the next is easier done through the division of labor and the use of equipment that has been designed to tackle individual tasks. The division of skilled labor eventually led to sustainable growth and became a precursor to mass production.

Self-love becomes the true motivation for an exchange in Smith which drifts away from the ethical or moral action and humanistic considerations that rationalized exchanges before. The division of labor should not be seen in isolation but in relation to the market. For example, in an isolated village, it might be insignificant to even consider a division of labor as the market is extremely small and the availability of talent in many areas is limited. On the contrary, in a big city where the market is extensive, it would be of value. Here, we also see how geographically concentrated populations can experience higher growth rates than distributed ones.

An issue that Smith addressed in his work is the difference between real or natural and nominal or market prices of commodities. As natural price (value in the context of this book), he considers the price of a commodity that "is neither more nor less than what is sufficient to pay the rent of the land, the wages of the labour, and the profits of the stock employed in raising, preparing, and bringing it to market, according to their natural rates". Unfortunately, the market price of a commodity is not constant and is regulated by the supply and demand for that commodity in the market: Natural prices. Demand in this case is not an effectual demand as it is regulated by the disposable income people can afford to satisfy their need.

A late contemporary to Smith was David Ricardo who advocated the creation of value through specialization at the country level to achieve comparable advantage. A country would capitalize on technology to produce something at a lower cost compared to other countries and then trade with them. In this way, international trade through the exchange of value could benefit all participating nations. The assumption has been that all countries can discover a technological edge and conflict would not arise. Unfortunately, at the time of Ricardo, England was experiencing the blockage of the Napoleonic wars, and the theory couldn't be justified in practice.

Ricardo explicitly discussed the concept of scarcity in his work, particularly in the context of rent theory and the distribution of income between landowners, capitalists, and laborers. In his theory of rent, which is based on the scarcity of land, he explained that rent arises because land is scarce and not all land is of the same quality. The best, most fertile land is limited, and as population grows, less fertile land must be used for agriculture. The difference in productivity between the most and least fertile land creates economic rent. This rent increases as the demand for agricultural products rises, due to the scarcity of fertile land.

Scarcity became the dominant feature in economic investigations during and after the Industrial Revolution of the Victorian era. Only when the economy begins to shift from scarcity to abundance and multiple choices become available to consumers can they appreciate scarcity later on. Civilization imprinted scarcity into consciousness, so a modern man can be considered as one who is civilized by virtue of his technology and the boundlessness of his desires. Poverty in this view is not seen as a contradiction to the modern or civilized human but rather as an inevitable condition of life. It was "normal" or acceptable for some to be poor.

Ricardo also addressed the concept of diminishing marginal returns, which is linked to scarcity. As more labor and capital are applied to a fixed amount of land (which is scarce), the additional output from each new unit of input decreases. This idea plays into the broader understanding of scarce resources and the limits of productive capacity. In his theory of comparative advantage, Ricardo also indirectly addressed the idea of scarcity by showing how countries benefit from specializing in the production of goods for which they have a relative advantage in resources, which are often scarce.

This issue though didn't prevent the development of the concept of diminishing returns. As the country was cut off from supplies of cereal grains (wheat, corn, rye, oats, etc.), it had to rely on its own limited production resulting in high prices. Out of fear that the end of the war will allow imports to resume and as a result lower the prices, the argument was made by those involved in agriculture that prices should stay high to ensure the competitiveness of the local production. In the opposite case, the local agricultural industry will suffer and deteriorate, and the land dedicated to cultivation will deteriorate and increase the shortage of cereal grains. Each additional plot of land that would be dedicated to cultivation will become more expensive to cultivate. To alleviate the situation, the government would have to impose high import duties to generate revenue for investment in the local agricultural industry. The goal of the opponents of the imposition of duties was to show that capital investments in agriculture were diminishingly efficient. For every amount of additional capital invested in the form of labor, the rewards would be diminishing making the duty-investments cycle unsustainable. The country would overall be better off importing cheap cereal grains.

Such "unorthodox" ones might say propositions proliferated those times including the radical view by William Spence that Britain could be reasonably prosperous even independent of commerce because the increasing prices will make more money for landowners who would be more inclined to spend it instead of spreading it to the hands of the monied classes who would tend to reserve it in savings. This view was countered by James Mill by the position that if the nation increases its annual production, it will be like it is enlarging its market and thus the demand will follow suit. For this to work, Thomas Malthus stated that one should ensure that the excessive planned savings or hoarding of the many does not exceed the planned investment. Otherwise, depression will follow.

Another questionable outcome of the thinking of the early 19th century was that supply can create its own demand. This was attributed to Jean-Baptiste Say and is often referred to as Say's law. The rationale was that a production process in itself will generate income, through wages, purchase of equipment and resources, rent, etc. that would eventually go back into the market as people will afford to buy more. So, the supply of one product could lead to the demand of another. Say believed that in a free market, there would not be a general glut or surplus of goods. Any temporary imbalances in supply and demand would be corrected by price adjustments, assuming there are no external barriers.

Say's law was challenged by John Keynes during the Great Depression when he argued that demand, not supply, drives economic growth and that insufficient aggregate demand could lead to prolonged periods of unemployment and underproduction, as seen in economic recessions. Clarity was provided by John Stuart Mill (the son of James Mill) who argued that the supply is at the same time demand is grounded on the assumption of a state of barter where the roles of seller and buyer are the same. You sell something to a buyer and at the same time you receive something, so you become a buyer for what the other person gives or sells you. If one treats money as a good, then the analogy is preserved logically. You give one good in exchange for another.

Mill also made a clear distinction between value and utility. He argued that while utility (usefulness) is necessary for something to have value, value itself is determined by scarcity and labor, not utility alone. The cost of production was seen as the determinant of the long-term value of goods, while in the short term, the value (price) of goods is determined by supply and demand. If demand exceeds supply, prices will rise, and if supply exceeds demand, prices will fall, but these fluctuations are temporary. For goods that are limited in supply (land, works of art, etc.), their value is determined by scarcity rather than the cost of production. In such cases, the price is set by what people are willing to pay rather than how much it costs to produce. Overall, Mill believed that value under the influence of various forces is primarily determined by the cost of production for reproducible goods and by scarcity for non-reproducible goods, with supply and demand influencing short-term fluctuations in prices.

The classical economic thought of value faced a lot of critique, especially from what is known as the Historical School (a 19th century movement rooted in Germany) that eventually led to the neoclassical view. A core issue was the assumptions of classical economics, better seen as political economics and, in particular, the failure to indicate a purpose. Additionally, it was perceived that it relied on deduction from simple postulates and neglected the institutional factor and the rate of mobility of capital and labor. To counter these issues, the Historical School emphasized the importance of the historical, cultural, and social context of economic systems and the need for empirical data in formulating theories. Wilhelm Roscher was one of the founding figures of the (older) historical school and advocated that economies and their perception of value evolve over time and this evolution should be considered for accurate economic analysis.

The Austrian School, led by Carl Menger, rose as a proponent of the Historical School with its view that empirical data are without significance and without theoretical foundations. According to them, the actions of individuals and subjective values should become the basis of economic analysis. The value of goods and services is subjective and arises from the importance individuals place on them to satisfy their needs and desires. In this respect, value is an inherent property of goods and services but an assigned one based on the circumstances that created the needs and wants of the consumer. Since individuals are different, and they face different challenges, value can vary significantly between them.

This kind of thinking gave rise to the concept of marginal utility for the individual as additional satisfaction or benefit he or she derives from consuming an extra unit of good or service. Based on this concept, diminishing marginal utility was defined as the decreasing value of a good or service as more is consumed. The individual eventually gets saturated and additional consumption adds zero value. In the end, the value of a good or service is determined by its marginal utility; the satisfaction of the least important need that the last unit of a good or service can fulfill. An ordering of goods can be considered based on their importance in satisfying human needs. Higher-order goods (such as flour, wheat, and farming equipment) become more important as they are needed to produce first-order goods like bread.

One misidentified or misunderstood figure by some in the neoclassical economic thought of value was Karl Marx. He was or is often identified with socialism and even communism due to his pure labor theory of value. With respect to labor, Marx was not any different from Smith in that he considered the ratios of labor time expended in the production of goods as the defining factor of their market price. This has nothing to do with a social process or any political system of the sort. It is a purely market perspective. Capital accumulation and land appropriation in that respect were acting as an inhibitor to the proper allocation of value to laborers.

Where Marx diverged was in his theory of wages. As value was determined by the labor cost of production, the value of labor was determined in the market by the labor cost of producing labor. Otherwise, the laborer and their dependents and obligations put together require some amount of "labor" (seen here as energy, capital, etc.) to be sustained physiologically and socially. So, the price a laborer should expect from the market for his work or contribution in exchange should be sufficient to sustain him and his dependents. Marx just saw this as an exchange of labor. When I put a certain amount of work or labor in a market, I would expect in exchange someone to reward me with a price that would have been produced by someone else's equal amount of work. But instead of exchanging work for work, we just exchange work for money. This is not different than the barter economies of the past where I would pay for the milk you milked from your cow with the salt, I collected myself.

While the rationale of many economists was just, they typically differ in how they treat human nature. For example, in Smith's view, the employer will always aim at minimizing cost by lowering wages to subsistence levels. This "unjust" trend will break up in a progressive society where employers compete with one another in acquiring skills and thus drive wages up. Marx, though, did not believe in a progressive society but in a deteriorating one and that wages will always be pushed down by the superior bargaining power of the owners of capital and the inability of the employees to act collectively in claiming their just wage. This would eventually lead, according to Marx, to a surplus of value which would be capitalized by the dominant social class. He went further to argue that since most of the surplus value was derived from investment in the employment of labor, the profit it produces is the result of the exploitation of value in the form of labor.

A contemporary of Marx (although much younger), in a radically different economic domain, was Alfred Marshall. Oftentimes, seen as a founding figure of neoclassical economics, Marshall focused on microeconomic principles including supply and demand, marginal utility, and the equilibrium of markets. He aimed to refine classical economics by incorporating mathematical analysis and emphasizing the role of consumers and producers in price determination. His views on value represent a comprehensive integration of demand-side (utility and marginal utility) and supply-side (cost of production and marginal cost) factors. He emphasized that value and price in a market are determined by the interplay of these forces at the time under consideration.

Mashall's economic thought influenced many, with prominent among them one of his students John Keynes who critiqued the classical value theory and Say's law. Keynes believed that aggregate demand (total spending by households, businesses, and the government) is not always sufficient to purchase the total output produced, leading to unsold goods and unemployment. This shifted the focus from supply-side determinants of value to demand-side factors with insufficient aggregate demand leading to prolonged periods of economic stagnation, regardless of the productive capacity or value of goods supplied.

While Keynes did not focus specifically on value, he did critique the classical view that is determined by supply and demand that were mostly based on the assumption of full employment. He departed from the view of marginal utility and the equilibrium between supply and demand and posed that equilibrium could even achieved when resources, particularly labor, were underutilized. Unemployment in this sense could be an acceptable part of a stable market.

Keynes focused on the value of money as influenced by broader monetary and institutional factors instead of just being the result of commodity exchange. Liquidity and purchasing power would reflect the value of money in a given state of demand in the economy. He introduced the concept of liquidity preference to represent the value people place on holding money for precautionary, speculative, and transactional reasons. This affects interest rates and, in turn, investment and aggregate demand, making the value of money and investments highly dependent on psychological factors and expectations about the future, not just supply and demand.

Value in economic activity according to Keynes was not just about objective utility or marginal production but was deeply influenced by subjective expectations and uncertainty. This is most evident in his discussion of investment decisions and the role of "animal spirits", where the value assigned to future income or investment returns depends on the confidence or pessimism of economic agents. Considering that rarely individuals, if ever, have perfect foresight or access to all information, Keynes emphasized the role of uncertainty in determining value, especially in financial markets. The value of assets, labor, or goods could fluctuate widely based on changing expectations about future conditions.

Many post-Keynesian economists picked up the concept of value from different perspectives. Joan Robinson added that value and pricing can be affected by monopolistic attitudes and firms in imperfect markets can manipulate prices. As a result of such actions, the value of goods deviated from their perfect market baseline. Milton Friedman was another prominent figure from what is known as the Chicago School of Economics who was a proponent of the free market and the reduced role of government in influencing value by intervention. In Friedman's work, the value of money and goods was tied to expectations of inflation and the long-term quantity of money in circulation. Controlling the supply of money was key to stabilizing prices. John Hicks finally focused on how markets reach equilibrium and how value is derived from the choices we make over time. Future expectations and choices would influence present value. The market environment in this way is seen as the adynamic exchange between the present and the future.

In the 20th century, economics though was represented by multiple schools of thought that either focused on specific aspects of economics or categories. Some theorists build on Keynes' ideas with the incorporation of the neoclassical concept. They posited that the economy can be stabilized using monetary and fiscal policies. Additionally, they considered market inertia as the reason for slow price adjustments that resulted in imperfect market operations. We also have the development of behavioral economics that challenge the assumption of rational behavior. Individuals are psychological entities where personality attitudes influence decision-making in changing environments. The individual often acts irrationally due to cognitive biases, emotions, and social influences. Modeling such behavior is difficult as only aggregate and simplified tendencies can be captured in mathematical formulas.

Another emphasis of modern times is on institutional economics where government and institutions act as controllers of value through laws, regulations, and proper oversight of the market. The belief is that economic behavior and outcomes are strongly influenced by social and political frameworks within which people operate. A derivative of this kind of thinking is modern monetary theory where countries can finance government spending by controlling their own currency (printing money is an example) instead of borrowing or raising taxes. As long as inflation is kept under control, the proponent of this theory argues that deficits can be sustained as long as they stimulate economic activity and reduce unemployment. Special attention is given to low- and middle-income nations that need economic growth to improve their standards of living. Social, political, and cultural factors need to be considered in economic analysis to address issues such as poverty reduction, inequality, and human development.

A modern consideration in economic thinking is the influence of the environmental challenges we now face. Environment and ecological economics has risen as a school of thought that focuses on the relationship between economics and the environment, emphasizing sustainability. It challenges traditional economic growth models, arguing that they are incompatible with finite natural resources and ecological limits. Concerns for the environment also gave rise to the emergence of biophysical economics as a response to the limitations of traditional economic models in addressing issues related to energy, resource depletion, and environmental degradation. It was influenced by earlier ideas in ecology, biology, and thermodynamics.

The key idea is that the economy is not just an isolated system of money and exchange, but it operates or exists in the physical world, subject to natural laws and environmental limits. Energy is viewed as the basis of economic activity as it is the foundational resource that drives all economic production. Since energy is required for extracting resources from the earth and building materials, as well as producing labor, capital, and technology, it is more fundamental than anything that is derived from its consumption. Without energy, no economic system can function.

The theory builds on the laws of thermodynamics, particularly the idea that energy is consumed (and often degraded) in every economic process. The efficiency of energy use is seen as crucial for sustainable economic growth. The theory also stresses the finite nature of natural resources, including fossil fuels, minerals, and water. It critiques conventional economics for assuming unlimited growth and neglecting the depletion of non-renewable resources. Ecological systems (such as forests, oceans, and the atmosphere) provide vital services to economies, such as absorbing carbon emissions or replenishing freshwater. Biophysical economics argues that the economy cannot grow indefinitely on a planet with limited resources and must adapt to these constraints.

One of the core metrics in biophysical economics is energy return on investment (EROI), which measures the amount of usable energy obtained from an energy source relative to the amount of energy invested to extract or produce it. For instance, oil production once had a high EROI (getting a large amount of energy for a relatively small energy investment), but as oil becomes harder to extract, the EROI declines. Low EROI energy sources (e.g., unconventional oil and solar) might require more energy investment, limiting their potential to support large-scale economic growth.

Despite its popularity as taking a high moral ground, biophysical economics has been criticized for catastrophizing and neglecting important factors like human capital, technological innovation, institutions, and entrepreneurship. The adaptability of markets, which can substitute scarce resources with alternatives through innovation and investment, argues that mainstream economists are not taken into consideration. For example, as fossil fuels become scarcer, new energy technologies (such as solar or wind) can emerge to maintain economic growth. Biophysical economists are seen as being too deterministic by focusing on resource limits.

Biophysical economists counter the arguments by accusing mainstream economists as to naïve and overoptimistic of the abilities of humans to overcome any obstacle faced in nature. While technological advances can improve the efficiency of resource

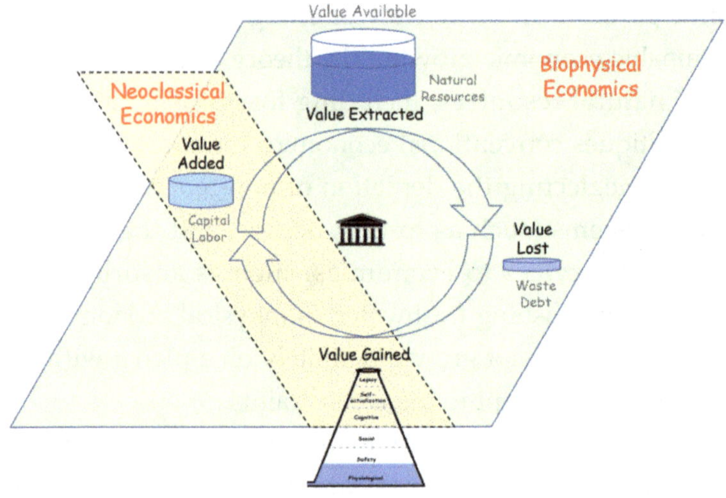

Figure A.1. The cycle of value from a historical perspective.

use, biophysical economists argue that technology alone cannot overcome the fundamental constraints of finite resources. They often critique the over-reliance on technology to solve environmental and resource challenges without addressing underlying physical limits. Considering all these arguments, the law of conservation of value as it is presented in this book aims to provide the foundation upon which various schools of economic thought can build their arguments in a formal and quantitative way.

The neoclassical economics examples that we saw in this book can be expanded to cover a more holistic view of economics as modern biophysical economics does. A view of the cycle of value in terms of both neoclassical and biophysical economics is presented in Figure A.1. In this view, the dynamic nature of the cycle becomes evident as the actors are in constant need of gaining value.

BIBLIOGRAPHY

Adelman, I. (1975). Development economics — A reassessment of goals. *The American Economic Review*, **65**(2), 302–309.

Altman, M. (2006). Human agency and free will: Choice and determinism in economics. *International Journal of Social Economics*, **33**(10), 677–697.

Anyanwu, U. M., Anyanwu, A. A., & Cieślik, A. (2021). Does abundant natural resources amplify the negative impact of income inequality on economic growth? *Resources Policy*, **74**, 102229.

Arrow, K. J. (1990). Economic theory and the hypothesis of rationality. In Eatwell, J., Milgate, M., & Newman, P. (eds.) *Utility and Probability* (pp. 25–37). London, UK: Palgrave Macmillan.

Arrow, K. J. (1996). The economics of information: An exposition. *Empirica*, **23**(2), 119–128.

Aumann, R. J. & Perles, M. (1965). A variational problem arising in economics. *Journal of Mathematical Analysis and Applications*, **11**, 488–503.

Baghaei Lakeh, A. & Ghaffarzadegan, N. (2016). The dual-process theory and understanding of stocks and flows. *System Dynamics Review*, **32**(3–4), 309–331.

Baumgärtner, S. & Quaas, M. (2010). What is sustainability economics? *Ecological Economics*, **69**(3), 445–450.

Bellofiore, R. (1989). A monetary labor theory of value. *Review of Radical Political Economics*, **21**(1–2), 1–25.

Ben-Ner, A. & Putterman, L. (eds.) (1998). *Economics, Values, and Organization*. Cambridge, UK: Cambridge University Press.

Benabbou, N., Chakraborty, M., Elkind, E., & Zick, Y. (2019a). Fairness towards groups of agents in the allocation of indivisible items. In *The 28th International Joint Conference on Artificial Intelligence (IJCAI'19)*.

Benabbou, N., Chakraborty, M., & Zick, Y. (2019b). Fairness and diversity in public resource allocation problems. *Bulletin of the Technical Committee on Data Engineering*. IEEE Computer Society.

Bénabou, R. & Tirole, J. (2016). Mindful economics: The production, consumption, and value of beliefs. *Journal of Economic Perspectives*, **30**(3), 141–164.

Benveniste, L. M. & Scheinkman, J. A. (1979). On the differentiability of the value function in dynamic models of economics. *Econometrica: Journal of the Econometric Society*, **47**(3), 727–732.

Bergemann, D., Bonatti, A., & Gan, T. (2022). The economics of social data. *The RAND Journal of Economics*, **53**(2), 263–296.

Bockstael, N. E., Freeman, A. M., Kopp, R. J., Portney, P. R., & Smith, V. K. (2000). On measuring economic values for nature. *Environmental Science & Technology*, **34**, 1384–1389.

Bowman, C. & Ambrosini, V. (2000). Value creation versus value capture: Towards a coherent definition of value in strategy. *British Journal of Management*, **11**(1), 1–15.

Brown, T. C. (1984). The concept of value in resource allocation. *Land Economics*, **60**(3), 231–246.

Brandenburger, A. M. & Stuart Jr, H. W. (1996). Value-based business strategy. *Journal of Economics & Management Strategy*, **5**(1), 5–24.

Broome, J. (1978). Choice and value in economics. *Oxford Economic Papers*, **30**(3), 313–333.

Cheshire, P. & Sheppard, S. (2017). On the price of land and the value of amenities. In *The Economics of Land Use* (pp. 315–335). Abingdon-on-Thames, Oxfordshire, UK: Routledge.

Colman, A. M. (2003). Cooperation, psychological game theory, and limitations of rationality in social interaction. *Behavioral and Brain Sciences*, **26**(2), 139–153.

Daoud, A. (2018). Unifying studies of scarcity, abundance, and sufficiency. *Ecological Economics*, **147**, 208–217.

Falk, A., Fehr, E., & Fischbacher, U. (2003). On the nature of fair behavior. *Economic Inquiry*, **41**(1), 20–26.

Fenwick, E., Steuten, L., Knies, S., Ghabri, S., Basu, A., Murray, J. F., Koffijberg, H. E., Strong, M., Sanders Schmidler, G. D., & Rothery, C. (2020). Value of information analysis for research decisions – An introduction: Report 1 of the ISPOR value of information analysis emerging good practices task force. *Value in Health*, **23**(2), 139–150.

Fischer, H. & Gonzalez, C. (2016). Making sense of dynamic systems: How our understanding of stocks and flows depends on a global perspective. *Cognitive Science*, **40**(2), 496–512.

Foley, D. K. (2000). Recent developments in the labor theory of value. *Review of Radical Political Economics*, **32**(1), 1–39.

Foley, D. K. (2004). Rationality and ideology in economics. *Social Research: An International Quarterly*, **71**(2), 329–342.

Foss, N. J. (1997). Austrian insights and the theory of the firm. In *Advances in Austrian Economics*. Emerald Group Publishing Limited.

Fukumoto, E. & Bozeman, B. (2019). Public values theory: What is missing? *The American Review of Public Administration*, **49**(6), 635–648.

Gagnier, R. (2000). *The Insatiability of Human Wants: Economics and Aesthetics in Market Society*. University of Chicago Press.

Grandmont, J. M. (1985). *Money and Value: A Reconsideration of Classical and Neoclassical Monetary Economics* (No. 5). Cambridge, UK: Cambridge University Press.

Grassl, W. (2010). Aquinas on management and its development. *Journal of Management Development*, **29**(7/8), 706–715.

Green, R. C. & Srivastava, S. (1986). Expected utility maximization and demand behavior. *Journal of Economic Theory*, **38**(2), 313–323.

Gronskas, V. (2003). Free choice in mixed economy: Types, their interaction and problems. *Management of Organizations: Systematic Research*, (26).

Hadziahmetovic, A., Halebic, J., & Colakovic-Prguda, N. (2018). Economic crisis: Challenge for economic theory and policy. *Eurasian Journal of Economics and Finance*, **6**(4), 48–55.

Hamilton, W. H. (2016). The institutional approach to economic theory. In *Alternatives to Economic Orthodoxy* (pp. 204–212). Routledge.

Hare, J. (2000). Scotus on morality and nature. *Medieval Philosophy and Theology*, **9**(1), 15–38.

Hicks, J. R. & Allen, R. G. (1934). A reconsideration of the theory of value. Part I. *Economica*, **1**(1), 52–76.

Horiuchi, S. (2015). Emergence and collapse of the norm of resource sharing around locally abundant resources. *Journal of Artificial Societies and Social Simulation*, **18**(4), 7.

Hursh, S. R. & Silberberg, A. (2008). Economic demand and essential value. *Psychological Review*, **115**(1), 186.

Johnson, V. (1939). Aristotle's theory of value. *The American Journal of Philology*, **60**(4), 445–451.

Jost, J. T., Blount, S., Pfeffer, J., & Hunyady, G. (2003). Fair market ideology: Its cognitive-motivational underpinnings. *Research in Organizational Behavior*, **25**, 53–91.

Kallis, G., Gómez-Baggethun, E., & Zografos, C. (2013). To value or not to value? That is not the question. *Ecological Economics*, **94**, 97–105.

Kauder, E. (2015). History of marginal utility theory. In *History of Marginal Utility Theory*. Princeton, NJ: Princeton University Press.

Lakdawalla, D. N., Doshi, J. A., Garrison Jr, L. P., Phelps, C. E., Basu, A., & Danzon, P. M. (2018). Defining elements of value in health care – A health economics approach: An ISPOR Special Task Force report [3]. *Value in Health*, **21**(2), 131–139.

Lewin, P. & Phelan, S. E. (2000). An Austrian theory of the firm. *The Review of Austrian Economics*, **13**(1), 59–79.

Li, X. & Hsee, C. K. (2021). The psychology of marginal utility. *Journal of Consumer Research*, **48**(1), 169–188.

Maxfield, S. (2008). Reconciling corporate citizenship and competitive strategy: Insights from economic theory. *Journal of Business Ethics*, **80**(2), 367–377.

Mazzucato, M. (2018). *The Value of Everything: Making and Taking in the Global Economy*. UK: Hachette.

Murtazashvili, J. & Murtazashvili, I. (2020). Wealth-destroying states. *Public Choice*, **182**(3), 353–371.

Myerson, R. B. (1992). On the value of game theory in social science. *Rationality and Society*, **4**(1), 62–73.

O'Donoghue, T. & Somerville, J. (2018). Modeling risk aversion in economics. *Journal of Economic Perspectives*, **32**(2), 91–114.

Orléan, A. (2014). *The Empire of Value: A New Foundation for Economics*. Cambridge, MA: MIT Press.

Patterson, M. (1998). Commensuration and theories of value in ecological economics. *Ecological Economics*, **25**(1), 105–125.

Pearce, D. W. & Pretty, J. N. (1993). *Economic Values and the Natural World*. London, UK: Earthscan Publications Ltd.

Piano, E. E. & Rouanet, L. (2020). Economic calculation and the organization of markets. *The Review of Austrian Economics*, **33**(3), 331–348.

Rabin, M. (1990). Communication between rational agents. *Journal of Economic Theory*, **51**(1), 144–170.

Reda, A. (2018). Abundance and scarcity: Neoclassical economic thought. In *Prophecy, Piety, and Profits* (pp. 51–58). New York: Palgrave Macmillan.

Resnick, S. A. & Wolff, R. D. (1994). Rethinking complexity in economic theory: The challenge of overdetermination. In *Evolutionary Concepts in Contemporary Economics* (pp. 39–59). Ann Arbor, MI: University of Michigan Press.

Rosenfeld, A. & Kraus, S. (2018). Predicting human decision-making: From prediction to action. *Synthesis Lectures on Artificial Intelligence and Machine Learning*, **12**(1), 1–150.

Sharma, A. K. & Kumar, S. (2010). Economic value added (EVA)-literature review and relevant issues. *International Journal of Economics and Finance*, **2**(2), 200–220.

Shogren, J. F. & Taylor, L. O. (2008). On behavioral-environmental economics. *Review of Environmental Economics and Policy*, **2**(1), 26–44.

Simon, H. A. (1979). Rational decision making in business organizations. *The American Economic Review*, **69**(4), 493–513.

Smith, V. L. (1976). Experimental economics: Induced value theory. *The American Economic Review*, **66**(2), 274–279.

Sneirson, J. F. (2019). The history of shareholder primacy, from Adam Smith through the rise of financialism. In *Cambridge Handbook of Corporate Law, Corporate Governance and Sustainability*. Cambridge University Press.

Spash, C. L. & Vatn, A. (2006). Transferring environmental value estimates: Issues and alternatives. *Ecological Economics*, **60**(2), 379–388.

Tennenholtz, M. (2002). Game theory and artificial intelligence. In *Foundations and Applications of Multi-Agent Systems* (pp. 49–58). Berlin, Heidelberg: Springer.

Van Staveren, I. (2013). *The Values of Economics: An Aristotelian Perspective*. Abingdon-on-Thames, Oxfordshire, UK: Routledge.

Vaughn, K. I. (1978). John Locke and the labor theory of value. *Journal of Libertarian Studies*, **2**(4), 311–326.

Veblen, T. (1909). The limitations of marginal utility. *Journal of Political Economy*, **17**(9), 620–636.

Viet, N. Q., Behdani, B., & Bloemhof, J. (2018). The value of information in supply chain decisions: A review of the literature and research agenda. *Computers & Industrial Engineering, **120**,* 68–82.

Viner, J. (1925). The utility concept in value theory and its critics. *Journal of Political Economy,* **33**(6), 638–659.

Williamson, O. E. (2005). The economics of governance. *American Economic Review,* **95**(2), 1–18.

Zhao, W., Wang, L., & Zhang, Z. (2019). Supply-demand-based optimization: A novel economics-inspired algorithm for global optimization. *IEEE Access,* **7**, 73182–73206.

INDEX